A Rape in the

A RAPE *in the* EARLY REPUBLIC

*Gender and Legal Culture
in an 1806 Virginia Trial*

ALEXANDER SMYTH

Edited and with an introduction by
RANDAL L. HALL

UNIVERSITY PRESS OF KENTUCKY

Scholarly publisher for the Commonwealth,
serving Bellarmine University, Berea College, Centre
College of Kentucky, Eastern Kentucky University,
The Filson Historical Society, Georgetown College,
Kentucky Historical Society, Kentucky State University,
Morehead State University, Murray State University,
Northern Kentucky University, Transylvania University,
University of Kentucky, University of Louisville,
and Western Kentucky University.
All rights reserved.

Editorial and Sales Offices: The University Press of Kentucky
663 South Limestone Street, Lexington, Kentucky 40508-4008
www.kentuckypress.com

Library of Congress Cataloging-in-Publication Data

Names: Smyth, Alexander, author.
Title: A rape in the early republic : gender and legal culture
in an 1806 Virginia trial / Alexander Smyth ;
Edited and with an introduction by Randal L. Hall.
Description: Lexington, Kentucky : University Press of Kentucky, [2017] |
Series: New directions in southern history | Includes index.
Identifiers: LCCN 2016046795| ISBN 9780813169521 (pbk. : alk. paper) |
ISBN   9780813169545 (pdf) | ISBN 9780813169538 (epub)
Subjects: LCSH: Deskins, John,—Trials, litigation, etc. | Hanson,
Sidney,—Trials, litigation, etc. | Trials (Rape)—Virginia—Tazewell
County. | Tazewell County (Va.)—History.
Classification: LCC KF223.D546 S69 2017 | DDC 345.755/02532—dc23
LC record available at https://lccn.loc.gov/2016046795

This book is printed on acid-free paper meeting
the requirements of the American National Standard
for Permanence in Paper for Printed Library Materials.

Manufactured in the United States of America.

Member of the Association of
American University Presses

Contents

Preface

On January 14, 1806, Sidney Major Hanson left the muddy trail she was following and climbed the steps into the home of Justice of the Peace Hezekiah Whitt. She was visibly distraught on this blustery day in their isolated neighborhood of Tazewell County, Virginia, deep in the Appalachian Mountains. Accompanying Hanson was her neighbor and longtime acquaintance John Deskins, on horseback. Deskins had joined her on this trip ostensibly to explain to Whitt slanderous statements that mutual acquaintances had made about Hanson. When they had started from Hanson's home, they were sharing the horse, and Hanson was carrying in her arms a book of law, *The New Virginia Justice* (1795) by William Waller Hening, which had been compiled to guide local officials such as Whitt in their work. But by the time they emerged from the woods, everything in their lives had changed. Only minutes earlier Deskins had raped Hanson on the rough gravel path. When they arrived at Whitt's, he was carrying the legal book and handed it to Whitt. As Hanson explained to Whitt that she had just been raped, despite threats Deskins had made earlier, she was starting down a complicated path through the justice system of the early republic.

We can only imagine the ways this traumatic violation of her body physically and mentally affected Hanson, a married white woman who was then about thirty years old, for the rest of her life. No documents record the many ways the rape surely haunted her. In fact, historians rarely are able even to show how early rape cases moved through the justice system. In this instance, however, because of a rare narrative of the trial of Deskins, a prosperous married white man, we can follow Hanson's

Illustration 1. Alexander Smyth, an ambitious attorney, politician, and military man, preserved the details of the trial of John Deskins. Smyth served as a brigadier general in the War of 1812. His record of leadership in an attempted invasion of Canada was widely considered disgraceful, but he nonetheless continued a successful political career after his time in the army. *Miriam and Ira D. Wallach Division of Art, Prints and Photographs: Print Collection, The New York Public Library. "Alexander Smyth, Brigadier General." New York Public Library Digital Collections. Accessed May 23, 2016. http://digitalcollections.nypl.org/ items/510d47da-fcd6-a3d9-e040-e00a18064a99.*

determined effort to bring her rapist to justice, first at the local level and then in the state's recently created district court system. Deskins soon admitted that sexual intercourse had occurred, and the question thereafter was whether it was consensual. The community scrutiny Hanson faced in that journey essentially put her on trial as well.

Alexander Smyth (1765–1830) was many things in his life: an immigrant from Ireland, a saltworks manager, a lawyer, a longtime Virginia state legislator, an inept army general in the War of 1812, and a six-term U.S. congressman. He was an ambitious man who liked to print his speeches for purposes of self-promotion. For that practice, historians can thank him. Nestled among his political speeches in a compilation published in 1811 is the narrative of Sidney Hanson's rape case, in which he served as a prosecutor. Smyth's telling of the trial explains the incident and its aftermath at a level of detail rare for a rape case, especially one in the South, so early in U.S. history.

This book reproduces Smyth's work in its entirety, and my introduction provides some necessary context and highlights various historical themes that the case illustrates and deepens. The introduction is not a comprehensive analysis of this document, however, and this book is offered in the hope that both students and scholars will use Smyth's work to bring new insights to many topics. Because Smyth was part of an adversarial legal process and represented one side in the trial, one cannot assume that he recorded every detail of the trial, but with the sort of critical reading that scholars routinely perform, the document can be of much use. Smyth had to acknowledge the defense's arguments in order to challenge them. It is my hope that the book will be a resource to anyone studying gender, law, and society in the early republic. Specialists on Appalachia and the South may be particularly interested, but the case is part of a national story of the coexistence of local legal customs and codified state law at a crucial period in the development of the U.S. legal system. Its depiction of the ideals that define virtue in women and men also speaks to national cultural trends.

To encourage classroom use, I have formulated potential discussion topics. And to further aid students, I have included some concise guidance on relevant additional reading materials; the studies listed there will also make obvious to scholars the sources of the ideas I use in framing the introduction. Otherwise, I have kept my editorial intrusion to a minimum; Smyth's spelling and punctuation have been retained throughout, and, with the exceptions noted later, italics and capitalization are as given in the original publication. Local records document the rape victim's name as Sidney *Hanson,* whereas Smyth uses *Henson.* In the introduction, I use *Hanson* because that is the spelling that endured in the family, but I leave Smyth's spelling intact in transcribing the document. This contrast between local usage and the printed record can serve as a subtle reminder of the dynamic process of local–state interaction in a time of only nascent standardization and bureaucratization. Throughout his explanation of the testimony in the case, Smyth used footnotes to document whose testimony supplied the point he was making. To create a simpler document, I moved those notes to the text as parenthetical references. I placed Smith's other, longer footnotes, marked by asterisks, in brackets within the text and set them in italics. I added the section labels within the text to aid navigation and created an occasional editor's note to clarify minor points. In addition, I reproduced a selection from Hening's work *The New Virginia Justice* that relates some of the common-law precedents and Virginia statutory wording about rape used in the case. Also appended is a selection from a book published in 1801 on the trial of Jason Fairbanks, convicted that year of murdering Elizabeth Fales, a young Massachusetts woman (Fairbanks claimed she committed suicide). Smyth mentions the case prominently in his argument to the jury in the Deskins case.

Introduction

On January 24, 1806, John Deskins came before the county court of Tazewell County, Virginia, deep in the state's mountainous backcountry. He was "charged with feloniously ravishing and having carnal knowledge with Sidney Hanson on the 14th day of January 1806." The justice system moved quickly. On January 25, "the prisoner was again brot to the bar, and on his final examination, the Court were unanimously of opinion, that he should be committed to the District Jail and there remain until the District Court holden at Washington Courthouse, for further trial."[1] In early May, a jury in the district court at Washington Courthouse (or Abingdon) convicted Deskins of rape and decided he should receive a sentence of ten years in the state penitentiary, the minimum allowed for the crime. The judge sentenced him to serve ten years, with at least two of those years to be in solitary confinement (p. 100).[2] The Tazewell County Court appointed Deskins's wife, Rebecka, and his brother, Stephen Deskins, to be trustees of his estate while he was in prison.[3] John Deskins was the only rapist to enter the state penitentiary in 1806. He was released in 1813, pardoned with two years, five months, and fifteen days remaining on his sentence.[4]

Deskins's trustees apparently took good care of his affairs while he was in prison. In 1806, they paid taxes on 425 acres of land. Deskins returned to Tazewell County after his release, and in 1814 he paid taxes on 505 acres.[5] Before 1806, both John and Stephen Deskins had served on juries in the local court, indicating the family's solid civic status.[6] John Deskins had been among the first to sign a petition to the state legislature in 1798 in which residents of Wythe and Russell Counties asked for the

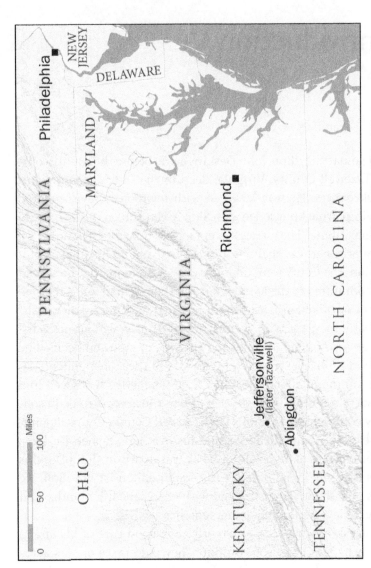

Map 1. Virginia, 1806. *Courtesy GIS/Data Center, Fondren Library, Rice University.*

formation of Tazewell County, which was created the following year.[7] Two spots above Deskins's name on that petition was the signature of David Mark Hanson, husband of Deskins's victim in 1806. The Hansons had immigrated to Virginia from Ireland and, like the Deskins family, were successful in acquiring land and good standing. David Hanson had served as a justice on the new county's first court, among other civic duties, and he owned an adult slave and more than 500 acres of land in 1806.[8] Despite Deskins's return to Tazewell County in 1813, the Hansons remained in Virginia. The census of 1850 shows seventy-five-year-old Sidney Major Hanson living in adjacent Russell County with one of their sons.[9]

The rape disappeared from memory. Genealogists do not write about it. The local historian transcribing the county order books for future researchers even changed the original wording of the indictment, "charged with feloniously ravishing and having carnal knowledge with Sidney Hanson," to the more decorous "charged with indulging in improper and unseemly behavior with Sidney Hanson."[10]

For the historian, this is where the story would normally end. Rape cases, in particular those in the colonial and early-republic eras, are notoriously difficult to research, and dates and terse official entries are often the only record.[11] The shame that attached to both perpetrators and victims led record keepers to retain only hazy documentation of a crime that many people preferred to ignore. A great stroke of fortune for the historian, however, allows for Deskins's rape of Hanson to be analyzed in much greater detail. At the district court, attorney Alexander Smyth, himself an Irish immigrant, represented the commonwealth as a prosecutor. Following the trial, a group of leading men in Abingdon promptly asked Smyth to write down "a report of [Deskins's] case as fully as you may be enabled" (p. 29). They recognized that the trial had "excited the most lively interest in the citizens, and brought into operation all the refined feelings of the heart, in favor of the innocent and unfortunate female, who fell a victim to an *infernal* plot" (p. 29, emphasis in the original). Smyth apparently obliged right away with his detailed recollections of the evidence given as well as with his closing statement to the jury and the judge's comments at Deskins's sentencing. The document he produced, titled "The Trial of John Deskins, in the Washington District Court, for a Rape. With the Sentence Passed on Him by Judge Holmes," was presumably published as a pamphlet, though no copies seem to be extant. It is preserved only because Smyth collected a number of his speeches and writings for a volume published in 1811, in which it takes up nearly a hundred pages.

Given that Smyth was a participant in the case, the historian must read his summaries critically; handled with care, however, this document opens a scholarly view onto a world seldom seen in such detail. That Smyth both helped win a conviction and inspired a group of local elites to ask that he prepare the arguments for print indicates at least a substantial community sense that his telling of the case here is credible.

Smyth's account of how an Appalachian community in the early republic handled this moment of crisis reveals a great deal about rape, gender relations, honor, violence, and, most obvious, the use of law and the courts at the time. Underlying all these topics is a county and a state teetering between the flexible community-based understanding of social order inherent in older legal approaches and the emerging centralized state government with its codified statutes and court procedures.[12] In 1806, however, both of these understandings of law gave great weight to reputation, and that topic ties together all the other factors highlighted in the narrative of this crime and trial. But even with this unusual material, the reader must still deploy a great deal of imagination to keep in mind Sidney Hanson's perspective on the violence against her.

Though the area's post–Revolutionary War influx of settlers had justified the creation of Tazewell as a county, its residents remained scattered lightly across an extensive rugged geography. The county's population of 2,127 in 1800 (of whom 1,908 were free persons) had grown to a total of 3,007 by 1810 (of whom 2,679 were free persons).[13] The Hansons lived on the "great road," a branch of the route that passed down the Valley of Virginia from Pennsylvania and extended toward Kentucky. David Hanson "some weeks" before the rape had embarked on a journey to Philadelphia for business, leaving behind a potentially vulnerable Sidney, their five young children, and an enslaved woman he owned (p. 32). The slowness of moving over long distances meant that travelers often stayed overnight with acquaintances, and neighbors kept an eye out for each other's welfare. John Deskins had even promised David Hanson that he would "bring a bag from mill, or the like, for his wife in his absence" (p. 52). It was not abnormal, then, that on Saturday night, January 11, 1806, two of the Hansons' former laborers, Frederick Trent and Henry Mash, and a recent tenant of the Hansons, James Bradley, traveled the mile from John Deskins's house, where they were drinking, to the Hansons' home, where they continued socializing and spent the night. The enslaved woman seems to have participated fully in the drinking and the fun of the evening, but this sort of social interaction between lower-class men and the enslaved was also not unusual, in spite of the unease it sometimes caused elite white men bent on maintaining the racialized order of a society with slaves.[14]

A social event mixing races and genders probably would not have occurred in a more elite household; however, these men were well known to Sidney Hanson. What was unusual, though, even in the rough-and-tumble world of impoverished laborers and slaves, was the directness of the sexual innuendo regarding Sidney Hanson, a white woman of a somewhat higher class, that circulated among the men before they arrived at the Hansons that Saturday. Bradley claimed to Trent and Mash that he had "had illicit intercourse with Mrs. Henson" (p. 32) and would do so again that evening. But Bradley became so drunk Saturday night that while he was sleeping

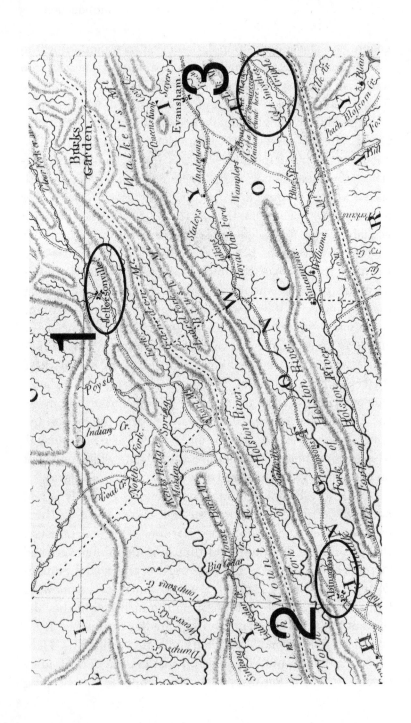

heavily, "Trent performed with a belt an odious and indecent trick upon him" (p. 33). Testimony differs on whether Sidney laughed and approved or fled the room, but the enslaved woman apparently aided in the "indecent and mischievous plan for tormenting Bradley" (p. 33). As this atmosphere of gaiety and heightened sexual awareness cooled on Sunday morning, Mash, approaching Sidney even before she rose from bed, and Trent made her aware of Bradley's claims about her lack of sexual fidelity. The men then left.

Everyone involved knew the high stakes of slandering a respectable white woman's reputation. On Monday, Bradley and the two others returned to the Hansons' home, where Bradley, according to Trent, "seemed deeply confused; wish'd he was dead; acknowledged it was a lie; said he'd give a lie-bill; and also offered two colts, supposed to be all his property, to be suffered to go clear" (p. 34). The three men then spent Monday night at the home of Deskins, who worried that Bradley would flee the region without repaying a debt he owed Deskins. It was a valid concern: landless whites facing legal trouble often moved to avoid prosecution. This concern that loose talk could drive a man from home brought Deskins into the story, and the four men together went back to the Hanson home on Tuesday, January 14. These four and another visiting man "commenced shooting at a mark, and drank some whiskey"

Map 2 (opposite). This 1807 map captures the setting for Sidney Hanson's rape and the subsequent trial of John Deskins. Jeffersonville, the county seat of Tazewell County, is the highlighted location no. 1. The Hanson and Deskins homes were nearby. Notice the rugged mountains and the Great Wagon Road branch passing down the valley and through the town. Location 2 is Abingdon, home of the district court at which the documented trial took place. Location 3 marks Alexander Smyth's interests in Wythe County, underscoring his importance in the region. Detail from "A Map Of Virginia Formed from Actual Surveys, and the Latest as well as most accurate observations, By James Madison, D.D. President of Wm. & Mary College." *Courtesy David Rumsey Map Collection, http://www.davidrumsey.com/.*

(p. 34) supplied by either Mash or the enslaved woman; afterward, they went inside the house to talk with Hanson. She was "uneasy" about the slandering remarks and "asked if there was any law by which she could get redress" (p. 35). Bradley's proposal showed that he had turned to the old method of achieving justice by personalized, negotiated settlement—he would pay all he had and swear to the community that his claims had been false. But Hanson wanted to take advantage of formal legal options; she entered the public arena in a way that belies the era's legal stipulations about women's dependence on their husbands in political and judicial matters.

A delicate mix of legal processes dictated what took place next. Virginia was among the states attempting to gather and codify the statutes scattered across many decades of legislative activity. Local magistrates called "justices of the peace," however, still served as the first point of encounter with the legal system, and their training was minimal. They applied community standards or common law as readily as they turned to Virginia statutes. David Hanson had served as a justice of the peace, and he owned a copy of William Waller Hening's book *The New Virginia Justice* (1795), which attempted to regularize expectations of justices and to provide them with an authoritative reference on the law.[15] Deskins and the others consulted "Hening's Justice" (p. 34), and Sidney decided to visit a local justice to get "something done" (p. 69) that Tuesday before Bradley could flee. She knew that the nearest justice, Hezekiah Whitt, did not even own a copy of the reference book, so she "took Hening's Justice along" (p. 35). Deskins and Mash agreed to accompany her to Whitt's residence, but after some discussion about whether it was necessary for both Mash and Deskins to accompany here, Mash left the two others, and Deskins and Hanson proceeded without him. To reach Whitt's, about a mile away, Hanson and Deskins, together on his horse, had to travel an isolated gravel path across a river and over a ridge. Along the way, Deskins raped her and threatened to kill her if she re-

Edwd Trabue

THE

NEW VIRGINIA JUSTICE,

COMPRISING THE

OFFICE AND AUTHORITY

OF A

JUSTICE OF THE PEACE,

IN THE

COMMONWEALTH of VIRGINIA.

TOGETHER

WITH A VARIETY OF USEFUL PRECEDENTS
ADAPTED TO THE LAWS NOW IN FORCE.

To which is added,

An APPENDIX containing all the moſt approved forms of
CONVEYANCING, commonly uſed in this country,
Such as Deeds, of Bargain and Sale, of
Leaſe and Releaſe, of Truſt, Mort-
gages, &c.—Alſo the duties of
a Juſtice of the Peace ariſ-
ing under the laws of
the United States.

By WILLIAM WALLER HENING,
ATTORNEY AT LAW.

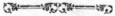

RICHMOND: PRINTED BY T. NICOLSON, 1795.

Illustration 2. In writing *The New Virginia Justice*, William Waller Hening sought to provide an up-to-date understanding of Virginia's law to justices of the peace, the local representatives of the justice system scattered throughout Virginia's communities.

vealed the crime. When they arrived at Whitt's, Deskins was astride the horse and carrying the legal book, and a distraught Hanson was on foot. Perhaps Deskins was hoping to intimidate her into silence, but Hanson was ready to seek redress for this physical violation that was far more serious than mere slander.

Hening's guidebook did not include directions precisely on how to handle allegations of slander. If the rape had not occurred and Hanson had convinced Whitt that Bradley had made slanderous statements about her, Whitt might have resorted to issuing a peace warrant or a warrant for good behavior against Bradley. The peace warrant was one of the most flexible tools available to help a justice of the peace maintain order. *The New Virginia Justice* explained, "Surety for the peace is one of the branches of preventive justice, and consists in obliging those persons whom there is probable ground to suspect of future misbehaviour to stipulate with, and give full assurances to the public that such offence as is apprehended shall not happen, by finding pledges or securities for keeping the peace." A similar principle was "surety for the good behaviour."[16] Justices of the peace thus had the discretion to take action against anyone they had reason to think might commit a crime or cause disorder in the future. Whitt could have forced Bradley to post a bond (or, more feasibly, find someone to do so on Bradley's behalf), which would have been forfeited if Bradley had disturbed the peace again. The imperative to keep the peace also was at the forefront of Hezekiah Whitt's mind when Hanson accused Deskins of rape.

Just as Bradley's instinct had been to negotiate a settlement rather than turn to the courts, Hezekiah Whitt reacted cautiously when Hanson reported her rape. Both Hanson and Whitt knew that Deskins might well swear he had not committed the rape and thus succeed, through perjury, in ruining Hanson's reputation instead of being brought to justice himself. Whitt offered to swear Deskins to secrecy, and Hanson cautiously agreed. Deskins had left the Whitts' house, but after they sent for him and he returned, he swore "he would not divulge the affair" (p. 41) unless she did. Without her husband by her side, Hanson, in spite of the violence against her, feared engaging in a battle of reputations in front of the community; Whitt's wife testified that Hanson's "object was to keep Deskins in peace, until her husband came home" (p.41). Peace in the community was the paramount goal of the older style of law that Whitt embodied, and Hanson needed reinforcements before publicly accusing Deskins.

Two days later David Hanson returned, and Sidney immediately told him the whole story. Despite David's own service as a justice, his immediate desire was to take his butcher knife and kill Deskins. Sidney pleaded for him "to desist" (p. 43), for fear of losing him; the slave "lock'd the door, and ran up the stairs with the key" (p. 43) to assist in keeping David at bay until he calmed down. The next day the Hansons worked with Justice Whitt and another justice of the peace to assemble Mash, Trent, Bradley, and others; after hearing everyone's story, the justices issued a warrant for Deskins's arrest. As Deskins was being escorted away from his home, David Hanson approached with his butcher knife, but this time he was restrained by the guard. Deskins was taken to Tazewell Courthouse, where various interested parties debated whether rape would be punished by death, as the ever-present copy of Hening's *Justice* indicated, or by confinement in the penitentiary, as a former member of the General Assembly authoritatively argued. An "examining court" at the county level heard the case on January 24 and 25. This court consisted of a group of the county's justices of the peace, serving as a panel to decide whether there was sufficient evidence to hold Deskins for trial at the higher district court level. As was longtime custom, a group of local women, rather than medical or legal professionals, examined Hanson's body, looking for and finding evidence of the violence and reporting back to the justices. Deskins was bound over for the trial at the district court in which Alexander Smyth served. There, a single, more highly trained judge would oversee the jury trial, and professional lawyers would engage in both the prosecution and the defense.

Hening's work had been first published in 1795; the legislation changing the penalty for rape from execution to a term of ten to twenty-one years of imprisonment for nonslave defendants was passed in 1796 (though slaves still faced execution if convicted of raping a white woman). This same reform act reduced the use of executions and corporal punishment for other crimes committed by whites in the hope that criminals could be reformed. As part of that optimism, legislators authorized the creation of a penitentiary in Richmond, one of the first in the United States, where hard labor, solitary confinement, coarse food, and other experimental techniques would be used to try to rehabilitate criminals.[17] Though Deskins was not on trial for his life, the stakes were nonetheless high for him.

As the case moved from the magistrate level to the county court and then to the district court, the interplay of customary and codified law continued. District courts had been implemented in Virginia in 1789 to bridge the vast gap between county courts, which handled all manner of local governance, and the General Court at Richmond, the state's highest court. Before that change, the distance involved in traveling to Richmond as well as the slowness of both the county courts and the overburdened General Court meant that state laws had less than the full force that the legislators hoped; justice often remained a localized affair. District courts were to serve as a more accessible and, to advocates of the developing state, more reliable way to try significant criminal and civil cases. As one historian explains, the new system had moved beyond "the idea that law ought to be concerned with investigating and enforcing the moral standards of a local community whose interests were homogeneous and whose overseers were the gentlemen justices of Virginia." Instead, "law, as opposed to antiquated notions of country justice, existed to enforce statutory prescrip-

I. *What it is.*
II. *Evidence on an indictment of rape.*
III. *Punishment of rape.*
IV. *Principal and acceſſary.*

I. What it is.

RAPE is an offence in having unlawful and carnal knowledge of a woman by force and againſt her will. But it
is ſaid that no aſſault upon a woman in order to raviſh her, however ſhameleſs and outrageous it may be, if it proceed not to
ſome degree of penetration, and alſo of emiſſion, can amount to
a rape; however it is ſaid that emiſſion is *prima facie*, an evidence of penetration. 1 *Hawk.* 169.

The offence of rape is no way mitigated by ſhewing that the
woman at laſt yielded to the violence, if ſuch her conſent was
forced for fear of death, or of dureſs. 1 *Haw.* 108.

Alſo, it is not a ſufficient excuſe in the raviſher, to prove
that the woman is a common ſtrumpet; for ſhe is ſtill under the
protection of the law, and may not be forced. 1 *Haw.* 108.

Nor is it any excuſe that ſhe conſented after the fact. 1 *Haw.*
108.

It is ſaid by Mr. Dalton, that if a woman at the time of the
ſuppoſed rape do conceive with child by the ſuppoſed raviſher,
this is no rape, for (he ſays) a woman cannot conceive except
ſhe doth conſent, and this he hath from Stamford and Britton,
and Finch. *Dalt. c.* 160.

But Mr. Hawkins obſerves, that this opinion ſeems very
queſtionable; not only becauſe the previous violence is no way
extenuated by ſuch a ſubſequent conſent, but alſo becauſe if it
were neceſſary to ſhew, that the woman did not conceive, the
offender could not be tried till ſuch time as it might appear whether ſhe did or not, and likewiſe becauſe the philoſophy of this
notion may be very well doubted of. 1 *Haw.* 108.

And L. Hale ſays, this opinion in Dalton ſeems to be no
law. 1 H. H. 731.

II. Evidence on an indictment of rape.

The party raviſhed may give evidence on oath and is in law
a competent witneſs; but the credibility of her teſtimony, and
how far forth ſhe is to be believed muſt be left to the jury, and
is more or leſs credible according to the circumſtances of
fact that concur in that teſtimony. 1 H. H. 633. For

Illustration 3. The entry on rape in Hening's *The New Virginia Justice* explains the crime using many references to English legal decisions.

tions, to execute speedy and efficient decisions on debt causes, and to prosecute serious criminals."[18] In referring Deskins to the county level for the attention of an examining court, Whitt was following the statutory procedure. That examining court then was tasked by the state law with deciding whether there was evidence of a felony that should be referred to the district court. The county court's decision to send Deskins to the district court reflected the seriousness of the allegations against him.[19]

That move does not mean everyone placed their faith in the young state system. While being transported to Tazewell Courthouse after his arrest, Deskins conferred with David Hanson, "offer[ing] him his effects, or any part of them only to give him a chance to run" (p. 44). Hanson refused, and Deskins then tried unsuccessfully to get the deputy sheriff to release him for a sum of money. After another vain effort to break free, Deskins again tried to bargain with Hanson, offering him "all he had in the universe . . . to make it up" (p. 46) and promising to leave the area. But the keeper of the tavern that was serving as Deskins's jail cell "told him the case was in the law," and so Hanson "could do nothing for him" (p. 46). Individual negotiations would not work now that the Hansons, at Sidney's wish, had brought the case into the formal state justice system. As another onlooker reiterated to Deskins, "[T]he case was in the law, and satisfaction could not be taken" (p. 45). Married women had little legal independence. Under the principle of coverture, a wife's property rights and other legal rights typically were united with and subordinate to her husband's. Referred to as "civil death," this common-law tradition changed only slowly in the nineteenth century.[20] Sidney nonetheless adeptly used the legal system to bring her attacker to justice. Deskins's options were now limited.

In his work for the prosecution, Smyth explicitly drew from the common law, but he also relied on Virginia statutes and simple parables from cases elsewhere in the United States. As one could expect from an ambitious professional working in a district court, Smyth attacked the lower levels of the Virginia judiciary by ridiculing Justice Whitt as incompetent in the case's early stages. In his closing remarks, though, Smyth used William Blackstone's famous work *Commentaries on the Laws of England,* first published in the 1760s, to organize his own arguments, thus underscoring that Virginia had not completely separated its judicial practices from older approaches.[21] Smyth explained, "Judge Blackstone, speaking of the evidence in the case of rape, has said; 'If the witness be of good fame; if she presently discovered the offence, and made search for the offender; if the party accused fled for it; these and the like are concurring circumstances, which give greater probability to her evidence'" (p. 64). But Smyth used a contemporary example when he cautioned the jury that Sidney Hanson had good reason to fear that Deskins might follow through on his threat to kill her. To make that point, the prosecutor explained a notorious Massachusetts case from 1801 in which a young man murdered the eighteen-year-old woman he was courting. "Who has not read the story of Jason Fairbanks, and Betsy Fales?" he exclaimed (p. 72).

The growth of print culture in the early republic is apparent in all phases of the Deskins case. Smyth relied on his listeners' having encountered press reports of a crime that had occurred many hundreds of miles away. The distribution and printing of books and newspapers, though most prevalent in the Northeast, had gradually spread to significant towns in all corners of the young nation, with broad implications. Community members might have queried Hanson's truthfulness because popular sentimental novels heightened readers' sense of the peril that seduction and illicit sex posed to respectable women. The routine use of books such as Hening's *The New Virginia Justice* and the fact that a local newspaper publisher was involved in the creation of Smyth's pamphlet on this case reflected both the demand for and the growing availability of printed material.[22] The technological and economic changes that aided the spread of print made it easier for the justice system to become more standardized and centralized, even as novels and news reports affected individual and community understanding of sexuality. Oral, face-to-face communication coexisted with print in the early republic.

Key to sorting out all the conflicting testimony and sources of law was local knowledge of character and reputation—of Deskins, of Sidney Hanson, and of their many witnesses. At the county court hearing, Deskins admitted having sexual relations with Hanson; thereafter, it was a matter of deciding who was more credible in the claim of force versus consent. Reputation was a jewel with many facets. In this high-stakes proceeding, Sidney Hanson was, metaphorically at least, on trial as well.

There were many contexts in which courts considered a defendant's community reputation when applying statutes or legal principles. Well-documented instances in Virginia range from determining the parentage of illegitimate children in the seventeenth century to investigating a possible infanticide within the prominent Randolph family in the 1790s. In the South, courts sometimes allowed reputable free blacks to file lawsuits against white people in spite of blacks' lack of legal standing.[23] Historians have, however, often focused on how the justice system balanced statutes against community standards in cases involving race and rape as well as consensual sexual interaction. How courts defined racial boundaries provides particularly clear examples of the muddled reality when law met circumstances.[24] As one historian concludes, "Race may have seemed fixed in law, but it was far more malleable in practice."[25] A court opinion from South Carolina in 1835 succinctly captures how this flexibility extended well into the nineteenth century:

We cannot say what admixture of negro blood will make a colored person, and, by a jury, one may be found a colored person, while another of the same degree of blood may be declared a white man. In general it is very desirable that rules of law should be certain and precise. But it is not always practicable, nor is it practicable in this instance. Nor do I know that it is desirable. The condition of the individual is not to be determined solely by the distinct and visible mixture of negro blood, but by reputation, by his reception into society, and his having commonly exercised the privileges of a white man. But his admission to these privileges, regulated by the public opinion of the community in which he lives, will very much depend on his own character and conduct; and it may be well and proper, that a man of worth, honesty, industry and respectability, should have the rank of a white man, while a vagabond of the same degree of blood should be confined to the inferior caste. It will be a stimulus to the good conduct of these persons, and security for their fidelity as citizens. It is hardly necessary to say that a slave cannot be a white man.[26]

Courts' flexible and sometimes even contorted attempts to define racial groups and to determine the credibility of witnesses by their community standing reached even into the twentieth century in litigation involving miscegenation and rape during the era of segregation. Class could define race, just as it could help establish witnesses' credibility. In a rape case in the early republic, with professional attorneys involved, a woman's character had to be assessed regardless of race.[27]

In the trial of John Deskins, both the prosecution and the defense mercilessly relied on prevailing assumptions about women's sexuality and the ingredients of good character. The courtroom itself was largely the province of men, so their vision of women held sway. The ideal of domesticity—that respectable women's special contributions were best made in the home— was becoming more powerful in the United States at this time.

Sidney Hanson's vigorous assertion of her desire for a public legal process defied this image of the woman on a pedestal, but in the end she was still judged by Smyth and the jury as to whether she met society's expectations for proper domestic feminine decorum.[28] In legal proceedings of the time, when a seemingly immoral, unchaste woman complained of rape, her testimony was likely to be dismissed as untrue. To convict Deskins, Hanson and the prosecutors had to prove her spotless reputation.

Deskins's many lawyers questioned Sidney Hanson's morality, arguing that "her agitation was probably feigned" (p. 86) and that her "riding in contact with [Deskins] upon the same horse, tended to create incontinent desires" (p. 59). The attorneys attacked her respectability with the allegation that she approvingly witnessed the lewd act done to the sleeping Bradley in her home, that "[s]he suffered drinking men about her house in her husband's absence" (p. 60), and that she allowed "Mash to sit at her bed side, while she lay in bed" (p. 60). She was also criticized for being jealous that her husband had committed infidelities. The prosecution in turn called "more than twenty of the most respectable persons residing in the county wherein she dwells, and in the counties immediately adjacent" to support the claim that Sidney Hanson was "one among the 'most respectable,' one of the 'first class' of women in our country" (p. 64). And her entire lifetime was at issue: "She is not only proven to have borne this character for the last ten years; but it has been proven that even in her childhood she was respectable. Her past reputation has been fully sustained" (p. 64). An important part of establishing Hanson's good character was demonstrating her active religious involvement as a Presbyterian while disproving the defense's allegations that she was a Roman Catholic and thus subject to suspicion. Churches were forums in which women established and defended honorable reputations. (If the trial had occurred a few years later, religion might have played an even greater role. The spread of evangelical religion to form the so-called Bible Belt across the South was in its early stages, and religious faith became ever more important to the definition of proper femininity.[29]) In contrast to Hanson's high standing, Smyth claimed, the women casting doubt on her reputation were, for example, "base" (p. 78) or "abandoned" (p. 78), adjectives commonly used in moral condemnation.

Racism intersected with gendered assumptions in the proceedings. The enslaved woman held by the Hansons had been a part of the story from the original carousing with the belt and a drunken Bradley, but her testimony does not appear in the recorded proceedings because slaves could not formally testify against white people. Whether she was consulted informally, as often happened at the local level in southern legal struggles, cannot be known because Smyth does not mention it. The enslaved woman did figure in the testimony in a second-hand way, though, as Hanson related how, as she was being attacked by Deskins, she pleaded with him "not to rob her of her chastity; and told him she would give him their negro girl, and all the property her husband owned, if he would let her go" (p. 36). And in an example more directly related to the court-room proceedings, Smyth drew on racist innuendo to try to discredit Aggy Harper and Molly Harper, women who had testified in Deskins's behalf. In this instance, though, Judge Hugh Holmes (former Speaker of the Virginia House of Delegates and a contributor to collecting and rationalizing Virginia's court decisions) worked to maintain the sanctity of the court procedure and resisted Smyth's attempt. Smyth "offered to prove, that by the general reputation of the country the Harpers are mulattoes; but that was refused to be admitted by the court" (p. 48). Court cases often hinged on the racial standing of a potential witness or litigant, and community definitions and recollections defined race.[30] Despite being rebuffed in his attempt to pursue that tactic, Smyth returned to the allegation in his closing remarks to the jury. He criticized the defense witnesses: "The dregs of mankind have been collected. Persons whom

no society, no *colour* will acknowledge, have been summoned"
(p. 77, emphasis in the original).

Considering social class was a significant part of evaluat-
ing character and credibility, although the lawyers of the early
republic sometimes had to present those assessments in a nu-
anced way for fear of offending sensitive jurymen in a time of
democratizing rhetoric. The defense argued to the jurors, "The
witnesses for the prisoner are decryed because they are poor . . .
and those for the commonwealth are selected because they are
wealthy" (p. 60). Smyth did in fact spend considerable time ex-
plaining the depths to which the laborers Trent, Mash, and
Bradley had sunk. For example, Trent was "a wicked, profligate,
abandoned, and immoral man," "a base licentious ruffian," "a
wretch," and "a man utterly destitute of decency, honor, and
virtue" (p. 80–81). Smyth asked the jury, "Can you give such a
man your confidence?" (p. 80). He even claimed that the three
were likely in league with Deskins to plan and then cover up
the crime. Smyth defended his use of testimony from leading
citizens with equal vigor.

In Smyth's closing arguments, the trial of John Deskins was
as much about the community and the other men in it as it
was about Deskins or his victim. The trial, according to Smyth,
had shown Sidney Hanson in the best light: "Here is the truly
honorable female character. A faithful, patient and affectionate
wife; a tender mother; a timid woman. Such is the female character we should cherish and protect" (p. 91). And if the court
failed to convict John Deskins, the men of Virginia would face
a hard choice the next time an honorable woman's character
was threatened. Would they respect the state's ability to protect chaste women? Or would they resort to lawless violence
that undermined orderly governance? Smyth proclaimed that
if justice could not be done by the courts, "The steel of the injured husband must drink the monster's blood. He will prefer
standing behind this bar as a criminal, to seeing his wife stand
before it, a disregarded, insulted witness. He will see that it is

the only course he can consistently with his wife's honor pursue" (p. 96).

Smyth could perhaps have dwelled even longer on the honor of men, but the truth was that David Hanson was not a model husband. During the trial, testimony had strongly indicated that David had at times been unfaithful in the marriage. Moreover, reminding the jury of his absence from home, which left his wife unprotected, would also have uncomfortably reminded the jurors that many men had to do the same thing to get ahead in the expanding commercial sector. Smyth nonetheless rose to rhetorical heights in urging the jury to make clear the law's ability to ensure the honor of virtuous men and women alike. "If you acquit the prisoner, and an injured husband shall hereafter imbrue his hands in the blood of the ravisher of his wife, when he shall stand arraigned at this bar for that offence, I shall not appear against him" (p. 97). Local mores might still trump the state's law if sexual honor were at stake.[31]

Seven years later, in 1813, John Deskins appealed to a different side of masculinity when he asked Governor James Barbour to approve his early release from the penitentiary. Petitioning the governor was a strategy prisoners often used, sometimes successfully. Deskins pleaded that his wife had recently died, his father-in-law was ill, and his brother, Stephen, who had been managing his estate, could no longer be of service. As a result, he explained, "if I am kept confined my dear children will be all bound out so that when I am at liberty I shall not have their loving company." He sought Barbour's sympathy by emphasizing the solace of family that men shared: "[Y]our Honour is at this time a husband and a father and I have no doubt but you must feel for a man in my situation."[32] The early nineteenth century was a time of rising importance for sentimental family bonds. Virginians embraced home and family with new emotional intensity.[33] Perhaps Barbour was moved by this argument, for Deskins was released and allowed to return to Tazewell County.

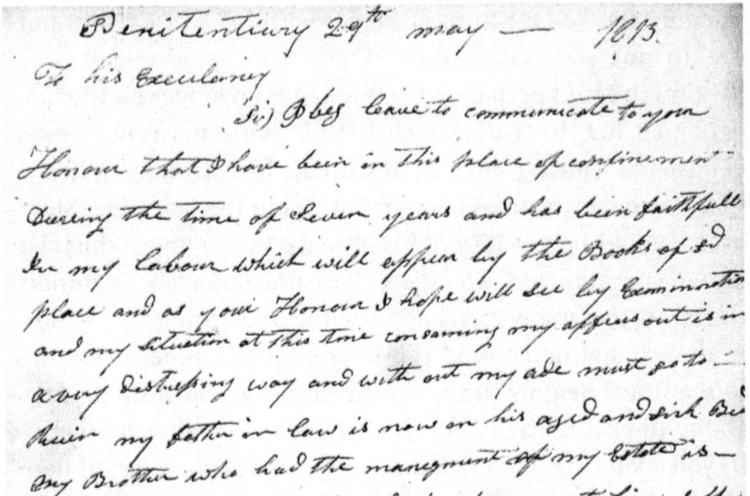

Penitentiary 29th may — 1813.

To his Excellency

Sir I beg leave to communicate to your
Honour that I have been in this place of confinement
During the time of Seven years and has been faithfull
In my Labour which will appear by the Books of sd
place and as your Honour I hope will see by Examination
and my situation at this time consarning my affairs out is in
a very distressing way and with out my ade must go to —
Ruin my father in law is now on his aged and sick Bed
my Brother who had the manegment of my Estate is —
be come so petified that he is of no use to him self
my wife has lately Died and if I am kept confined
my dear children will be all bound out so that when I am
at Libaty I shall not have Ther loving company your —
Honour is at this time a husband and a father and I have
no daubt but you must feel for a man in my
situation when fully known to your honour These
are the facts of my situation and I pray ~~you~~
your honours friendship and ade I am your most
and most obedient humble Servant

John Diskins

Illustration 4. In May 1813 John Deskins successfully appealed to Governor James Barbour for a pardon. Deskins explained that his wife had died and his children would soon be dispersed if he remained in the penitentiary. *John Deskins to James Barbour, May 29, 1813, in Box 7, Governor's Office (RG# 3), James Barbour Executive Papers, Accession 41557, State Records Collection (Library of Virginia, Richmond), microfilm, miscellaneous reel 5512, frame 704.*

This rare narrative of a rape trial opens up to us a Janus-faced community. It was an isolated place where an elderly justice tried to broker a bond of silence between a rapist and his victim, yet it was also thoroughly part of the literate, bustling early republic, as shown by David Hanson's trip to Philadelphia and Smyth's assumption that his listeners would know about both the English jurist Blackstone and a recent murder case in Massachusetts. We can note how much present legal procedures have changed, with today's guarantees of counsel and prohibitions of both hearsay evidence and attorneys' racist, sexist, or religiously chauvinistic rhetoric. But with every rape case that makes the news today, one is reminded of the ongoing importance of reputation and credibility and local biases. Perhaps the *overt* examples of how attacking women's choices and values worked both for and against Sidney Hanson can make all of us more aware of the often *covert* ways such processes play out in assessments of credibility in today's judicial system.

The very existence of this record must be credited to the elite white men of Abingdon, who saw in the case the possibility of influencing their growing community's political and cultural development. The case was to be an object lesson in public morality. Among those asking Smyth to prepare the narrative, for example, was John G. Ustick, who established the first newspaper in Abindgon, thus embedding the town in the early republic's print culture. Smyth agreed to deliver the manuscript to Ustick upon completion.[34] Smyth structured his pamphlet to thoroughly capture the proceedings. It first reproduces his exchange with the men who invited him to prepare it for publication. It then explains the testimony of the full array of witnesses, carefully documenting who made each important statement because the credibility of the witnesses was integral to the arguments. This explanation is followed by a reproduction of Smyth's lengthy argument to the jury, summarizing why Deskins should be found guilty. The narrative closes with the sentencing of Deskins, giving the judge final say in the text as in the courtroom.

Notes

1. Tazewell County Order Book, entries for January 24 and 25, 1806, p. 207, Tazewell County Records, microfilm, reel 11, Library of Virginia, Richmond.

2. Page numbers inserted parenthetically in the text refer to this current edition based on Alexander Smyth, "The Trial of John Deskins, in the Washington District Court, for a Rape. With the Sentence Passed on Him by Judge Holmes," in *Speeches Delivered by Alexander Smyth, in the House of Delegates, and at the Bar* (Richmond, Va.: Samuel Pleasants, 1811), 110–208. The period in solitary confinement was listed as twenty-seven months in *Report of the Joint Committee Appointed to Examine the State of the Penitentiary Institution, and Accompanying Documents* (Richmond, Va.: Thomas Ritchie, 1827), 11.

3. Tazewell County Order Book, 216.

4. *Report of the Joint Committee Appointed to Examine the State of the Penitentiary Institution*, 11, 22.

5. Netti Schreiner-Yantis, ed., *Archives of the Pioneers of Tazewell County, Virginia* (Springfield, Va.: n.p., 1973), 126, 142.

6. Ibid., 41, 42, 44,

7. Ibid., 296.

8. Ibid., 1, 123, 127; William C. Pendleton, *History of Tazewell County and Southwest Virginia, 1748–1920* (Richmond, Va.: W. C. Hill, 1920), 475.

9. Manuscript Census Returns, Seventh Census of the United States, 1850, Russell County, Virginia, District 54, Population Schedule, National Archives Microfilm Series M-432, reel 975, p. 239, National Archives, Washington, D.C. This census entry is the basis of my estimate in the preface that Sidney Hanson was about thirty years old at the time of the rape.

10. Schreiner-Yantis, *Archives of the Pioneers of Tazewell County*, 63.

11. There are a few similar narratives for cases around this time in New England and New York. See a discussion of them in Sharon Block, *Rape and Sexual Power in Early America* (Chapel Hill: University of North Carolina Press, 2006), 204–7.

12. A. G. Roeber, *Faithful Magistrates and Republican Lawyers: Creators of Virginia Legal Culture, 1680–1810* (Chapel Hill: University of North Carolina Press, 1981); Laura F. Edwards, *The People and Their Peace:*

Legal Culture and the Transformation of Inequality in the Post-revolutionary South (Chapel Hill: University of North Carolina Press, 2009).

13. Historical Census Browser, University of Virginia Library, at http://mapserver.lib.virginia.edu/index.html.

14. David Brown, "A Vagabond's Tale: Poor Whites, Herrenvolk Democracy, and the Value of Whiteness in the Late Antebellum South," *Journal of Southern History* 79 (November 2013): 799–840; Jeff Forret, *Race Relations at the Margins: Slaves and Poor Whites in the Antebellum Southern Countryside* (Baton Rouge: Louisiana State University Press, 2006); Charles C. Bolton and Scott P. Culclasure, eds., *The Confessions of Edward Isham: A Poor White Life of the Old South* (Athens: University of Georgia Press, 1998); Victoria E. Bynum, *Unruly Women: The Politics of Social and Sexual Control in the Old South* (Chapel Hill: University of North Carolina Press, 1992). Citizens of the early republic consumed alcohol at a remarkably high level on average (W. J. Rorabaugh, *The Alcoholic Republic: An American Tradition* [New York: Oxford University Press, 1979] , 8).

15. William Waller Hening, ed., *The New Virginia Justice: Comprising the Office and Authority of a Justice of the Peace, in the Commonwealth of Virginia. Together with a Variety of Useful Precedents Adapted to the Laws Now in Force . . .* (Richmond, Va.: T. Nicolson, 1795), 355–60. On the importance of Hening's work, see Roeber, *Faithful Magistrates and Republican Lawyers*, 217–18.

16. Hening, *New Virginia Justice*, 429, 439.

17. Samuel Shepherd, ed., *The Statutes at Large of Virginia, from October Session 1792, to December Session 1806, Inclusive*, vol. 2 (Richmond, Va.: Samuel Shepherd, 1835), 5–6; Philip J. Schwarz, *Twice Condemned: Slaves and the Criminal Laws of Virginia, 1705–1865* (Baton Rouge: Louisiana State University Press, 1988), 206; Paul W. Keve, *The History of Corrections in Virginia* (Charlottesville: University Press of Virginia, 1986), chaps. 1 and 2.

18. Roeber, *Faithful Magistrates and Republican Lawyers*, 216.

19. On the creation and role of district courts in cases of this sort, see William Waller Hening, ed., *The Statutes at Large; Being a Collection of All the Laws of Virginia, from the First Session of the Legislature, in the Year 1619*, vol. 12 (Richmond, Va.: George Cochran, 1823), 754–55, and Roeber, *Faithful Magistrates and Republican Lawyers*, 216.

20. Suzanne Lebsock, *The Free Women of Petersburg: Status and Culture in a Southern Town, 1784–1860* (New York: Norton, 1984), 23, 32–33; Cynthia Kierner, *Beyond the Household: Women's Place in the Early South, 1700–1835* (Ithaca, N.Y.: Cornell University Press, 1998), 125–26. For an ex-

ample of the gradual reform of coverture in the early republic, see Woody Holton, "Equality as Unintended Consequence: The Contracts Clause and the Married Women's Property Acts," *Journal of Southern History* 81 (May 2015): 313–40.

21. On the matter of rape, William Blackstone (1723–1780) himself was drawing from the work of seventeenth-century English jurist Matthew Hale (1609–1676).

22. Jack Larkin, "'Printing Is Something Every Village Has in It': Rural Printing and Publishing," in *A History of the Book in America*, vol. 2: *An Extensive Republic: Print, Culture, and Society in the New Nation, 1790–1840*, edited by Robert A. Gross and Mary Kelley (Chapel Hill: University of North Carolina Press, 2010), 145–60; John L. Brooke, "Print and Politics," in Gross and Kelley, *An Extensive Republic*, 179–90; Robert A. Gross, "Reading for an Extensive Republic," in Gross and Kelley, *An Extensive Republic*, 516–44; Cynthia A. Kierner, *Scandal at Bizarre: Rumor and Reputation in Jefferson's Virginia* (New York: Palgrave Macmillan, 2004), chap. 3; Jennifer Rae Greeson, *Our South: Geographic Fantasy and the Rise of National Literature* (Cambridge, Mass.: Harvard University Press, 2010), 104–11; Block, *Rape and Sexual Power in Early America*.

23. John Ruston Pagan, *Anne Orthwood's Bastard: Sex and Law in Early Virginia* (New York: Oxford University Press, 2003); Kierner, *Scandal at Bizarre*; Kimberly Welch, "Black Litigiousness and White Accountability: Free Blacks and the Rhetoric of Reputation in the Antebellum Natchez District," *Journal of the Civil War Era* 5 (September 2015): 372–98. Also see Eva Sheppard Wolf, *Almost Free: A Story about Family and Race in Antebellum Virginia* (Athens: University of Georgia Press, 2012).

24. Martha Hodes, *White Women, Black Men: Illicit Sex in the Nineteenth-Century South* (New Haven, Conn.: Yale University Press, 1997); Kirsten Fischer, "'False, Feigned, and Scandalous Words': Sexual Slander and Racial Ideology among Whites in Colonial North Carolina," in *The Devil's Lane: Sex and Race in the Early South*, edited by Catherine Clinton and Michele Gillespie (New York: Oxford University Press, 1997), 139–53; Joshua D. Rothman, *Notorious in the Neighborhood: Sex and Families across the Color Line in Virginia, 1787–1861* (Chapel Hill: University of North Carolina Press, 2003), chap. 4; Diane Miller Sommerville, *Rape and Race in the Nineteenth-Century South* (Chapel Hill: University of North Carolina Press, 2004).

25. Rothman, *Notorious in the Neighborhood*, 69.

26. *State v. Vinson J. Cantey* (1835), in *Reports of Cases at Law, Argued and Determined in the Court of Appeals of South Carolina*, 3 vols. (Charleston, S.C.: McCarter, 1857), 2:279.

27. Lisa Lindquist Dorr, *White Women, Rape, and the Power of Race in Virginia, 1900–1960* (Chapel Hill: University of North Carolina Press, 2004); Michelle Brattain, "Miscegenation and Competing Definitions of Race in Twentieth-Century Louisiana," *Journal of Southern History* 71 (August 2005): 621–58.

28. Kierner, *Beyond the Household;* Stephanie McCurry, *Masters of Small Worlds: Yeoman Households, Gender Relations, and the Political Culture of the Antebellum South Carolina Low Country* (New York: Oxford University Press, 1995).

29. John B. Boles, *The Great Revival: Beginnings of the Bible Belt,* new ed. (Lexington: University Press of Kentucky, 1996); Chris Beneke, "'Not by Force or Violence': Religious Violence, Anti-Catholicism, and Rights of Conscience in the Early National United States," *Journal of Church and State* 54 (March 2012): 5–32; Robert Elder, "A Twice Sacred Circle: Women, Evangelicalism, and Honor in the Deep South, 1784–1860," *Journal of Southern History* 78 (August 2012): 579–614; Robert Elder, *The Sacred Mirror: Evangelicalism, Honor, and Identity in the Deep South, 1790–1860* (Chapel Hill: University of North Carolina Press, 2016).

30. Hodes, *White Women, Black Men,* chap. 5; Rothman, *Notorious in the Neighborhood,* chap. 6.

31. On honor, see Bertram Wyatt-Brown, *Southern Honor: Ethics and Behavior in the Old South* (New York: Oxford University Press, 1982); Elder, "Twice Sacred Circle"; and David T. Moon Jr., "Southern Baptists and Southern Men: Evangelical Perceptions of Manhood in Nineteenth-Century Georgia," *Journal of Southern History* 81 (August 2015): 563–606.

32. John Deskins to James Barbour, May 29, 1813, Box 7, Governor's Office, Record Group 3, James Barbour Executive Papers, Accession 41557, microfilm, miscellaneous reel 5512, frame 704, State Records Collection, Library of Virginia, Richmond.

33. Kierner, *Beyond the Household,* chap. 5, esp. 168–70; Jan Lewis, *The Pursuit of Happiness: Family and Values in Jefferson's Virginia* (New York: Cambridge University Press, 1983).

34. Lewis Preston Summers, *History of Southwest Virginia, 1746–1786, Washington County, 1777–1870* (Richmond, Va.: J. L. Hill, 1903), 634.

Alexander Smyth, "The Trial of John Deskins, in the Washington District Court, for a Rape. With the Sentence Passed on Him by Judge Holmes," in *Speeches Delivered by Alexander Smyth, in the House of Delegates, and at the Bar* (Richmond, Va.: Samuel Pleasants, 1811), 110–208.

The Invitation to Publish

At a meeting of a number of citizens at Mr. James Allen's tavern, in Abingdon, on the evening of the 13th of May, 1806, the following address was unanimously adopted and presented to Col. Alexander Smyth, by David Campbell, and William Trigg, gentlemen, appointed by the meeting a committee for that purpose:

Abingdon, May 13, 1806

SIR,

THE trial of John Deskins, who was this day sentenced to ten years confinement in the jail and penitentiary house, having from the enormity of the crime of which he was convicted, and the very extraordinary circumstances attending it, excited the most lively interest in the citizens, and brought into operation all the refined feelings of the heart, in favor of the innocent and unfortunate female, who fell a victim to an *infernal* plot: we take the liberty to request that you will favor the public with a report of his case as fully as you may be enabled. This request is made, sir, with the more confidence, as we are persuaded, from the high opinion entertained by your fellow citizens of your talents and virtues, they will place great reliance on the impartiality of whatever you may lay before them.

With our best wishes for your welfare,

We remain, sir,
Your obedient servants,

MICHAEL DECKARD,	WILLIAM ALLEN,
JOHN GOLD,	WILLIAM KING,
SAMUEL GLEN,	CONNALLY FINDLAY,
STEPHEN TRIGG,	JOHN MCCORMICK,
WILLIAM TRIGG,	ROBERT CAMPBELL,
JOHN G. USTICK,	SAMPSON MOORE,
JONATHAN SPYKER,	JAMES WITHROW,
JAMES ALLEN,	EDWARD CAMPBELL,
ANDREW RUSSELL,	WILLIAM POSTON,
DAVID CAMPBELL,	WILLIAM CAMPBELL,
JOHN ALLEN,	

To Col. ALEXANDER SMYTH.

To which he returned the following answer:
*Abingdon, May 14, 1806.*GENTLEMEN,
THE lively interest felt by the citizens on the trial of John Deskins, is an evidence of their attachment to innocence, to virtue and to justice. By any act of mine to aid in confirming that attachment, would give me the most exqu[i]site delight. With that view, and to warn the chaste matron and modest virgin of the dangers to which want of caution may expose them, I will make a brief statement of the evidence in this case, extend the notes from which I addressed the jury, and furnish Mr. Ustick with the manuscript for publication.

The address of which you have been the bearers, is to me most grateful, as proceeding from men, who themselves members of an enlightened and virtuous society, are among that society's ornaments. To deserve the opinion therein mentioned, shall be my ambition.

Your most obedient,
ALEXANDER SMYTH.
Messrs. David Campbell and William Trigg.}

The Testimony

TRIAL OF JOHN DESKINS, &C.

TAZEWELL COUNTY, *to wit:*

THE jurors of the grand jury empannelled for the district composed of the counties of Washington, Wythe, Russell, Lee, Grayson and Tazewell, upon their oath present, that John Deskins, of the county of Tazewell aforesaid, husbandman, on the fourteenth day of January, in the year of our Lord one thousand eight hundred and six, and of the commonwealth the thirtieth, at the county of Tazewell aforesaid, and within the jurisdiction of the superior court appointed to be holden at Washington courthouse for the district aforesaid, with force and arms, in and upon one *Sidney Henson,* spinster, in the peace of God and of the commonwealth then and there being, violently and feloniously did make an assault, and her the said *Sidney Henson,* against the will of her the said *Sidney Henson,* then and there *feloniously* did ravish and carnally know, against the form of the statute in that case made and provided, and against the peace and dignity of the commonwealth. [*Editor's note:* In nineteenth-century legal usage, the word *spinster* was "the common title by which a woman without rank or distinction is designated." The word *husbandman* typically referred to a landowning farmer.]

ON calling the venire the prisoner challenged eight and elected four of them. [*Editor's note:* A *venire* is a panel of potential jurors.]

The commonwealth's counsel then offered to challenge three of those four for cause. The prisoner's counsel objected that it was then too late, as they were elected by the prisoner:

but the court decided the challenge for the commonwealth was made at the proper time.

The commonwealth's counsel challenged Samuel Laird, and asked him if he had not delivered an opinion that the prisoner ought to be acquitted. He said that after the trial before the examining court, at which he heard all the witnesses sworn, except Mrs. Henson, and after her testimony had been stated to him by one who heard it, he had said, that unless he heard something more, he saw no reason why the prisoner should not be acquitted.

The court decided that as the juror had not himself heard all the witnesses before he gave that opinion, and as he swore he was not prejudiced, he ought to be sworn; and he was sworn on the jury.—*Quere.*

From the evidence given in the case of John Deskins, *convicted of a rape committed on the body of Mrs.* Sidney Henson, *the wife of* David Henson, *esq. of Tazewell county, the following statement results:*

On Saturday the 11th of January, 1806, Frederick Trent and Henry Mash, who had been labourers at the farm of David Henson, and James Bradley who had made a crop there the preceding season, were drinking at the house of John Deskins, distant from the house of David Henson about one mile. Mr. Henson had been for some weeks absent from home on a journey to Philadelphia. His wife, five small children and a young negro woman, composed his family; and James Bradley had sometimes staid there. On that day, Bradley informed Trent and Mash that he had illicit intercourse with Mrs. Henson. When he told this to Trent, he was intoxicated (Trent). Mash thought him sober (Mash). [*Editor's note:* The names in parentheses indicate whose testimony Smyth is citing for the statement given. These names originally appeared as footnotes in Smyth's pamphlet.] That evening those three men went to Mr. Henson's house, and Bradley told the other two that he would that night go to bed to Mrs. Henson, and convince them of what he had said. No liquor was kept at Henson's; but Mash had some there at that time; and when they went there, Bradley got very drunk, and lay down and slept. While he lay in that situation, Trent performed with a belt an odious and indecent trick upon him (Trent). Mrs. Henson was present, and as to her conduct on discovering it, there was some contradiction in the testimony. A few days after the transaction, Trent and Mash in relating it said that as soon as Mrs. Henson discovered what was done, she ran out of that room (Brown, junior), and remained in another until the time of going to bed (John Davis): But Trent now swore that Mrs. Henson laughed at the trick. Half a gallon of whiskey was promised to the negro woman to aid in an indecent and mischievous plan for tormenting Bradley (Trent). Trent now swore that upon application being made to Mrs. Henson for her consent, she told the negro to do it, and that she would give a handkerchief for the half gallon of whiskey: But a few days after the transaction, Trent related that Mrs. Henson after she ran into the other room was asked if she would not give the negro a handkerchief for half a gallon of whiskey, and replied that she would (Brown, jun.). Trent also swore that while she was in the other room, and during the indecent exhibition, he went in, and found her at the door, looking on. In relating the same transaction a few days after it happened, he said he found Mrs. Henson standing at the door, and could not tell whether she was looking on or not (John Davis).

On Sunday morning, before Mrs. Henson arose from bed, Mash and Trent came down stairs, and Mash addressing himself to the negro, said there would be "cruel lawing when Mr. Henson came home" (Mrs. Henson). Mrs. Henson enquired about what; and Mash, setting by her bed side (Trent), informed her that Bradley had been talking disrespectfully of her, and said he would get Trent to tell her wherein (Mash). Trent did afterwards tell her, perhaps the same morning (Mrs. Henson).

In what manner Deskins, Trent, Mash, and Bradley spent

Sunday, or where they staid on Sunday night, does not appear from the notes of the evidence. On Monday they were together at one Owen's, and came from there in the evening to the house of Mr. Henson. The slander said to have been propagated by Bradley of Mrs. Henson was mentioned: Bradley seemed deeply confused; wish'd he was dead; acknowledged it was a lie; said he'd give a lie-bill; and also offered two colts, supposed to be all his property, to be suffered to go clear (Trent). From the house of Henson those four men went together to the house of Deskins, where they staid all night. There a real or pretended controversy arose between Deskins and Bradley about some balance claim'd by Deskins; and it being apprehended Bradley would run away, on account of the slander he had spoken of Mrs. Henson, Deskins threatened to get an attachment against him (Trent). On Monday morning they all proceeded once more to the house of Mr. Henson; but as they went, when they got to the barn of Deskins, he turn'd off to go to the house of Hezekiah Whitt, a justice, as Trent testified, but was persuaded to go along, Mash and Trent promising to endeavor to prevail on Bradley to compromise with him. Trent also said his own reason for wishing Deskins to go to the house of Henson was to be a witness of the delivery, by Bradley, of an oat-stack to himself. The four came together to the house of Henson. They there commenced shooting at a mark, and drank some whiskey furnished by Mash, or the negro woman; (three pints or half a gallon as Trent said; three half pints, as Mash said) which whiskey was drank by those four men and one Presley Davis who happened there. They came into the house, and fell into conversation concerning the slander Bradley had spoken of Mrs. Henson (Trent). She appeared uneasy about the report (Mash); and asked if there was any law by which she could get redress. Trent got Hening's Justice, and read a passage he supposed to apply. Deskins mentioned some other point of law (Trent). Deskins and Trent both advised her to have Bradley taken (Mash); and Trent told her Bradley was expected to leave the country immediately (Trent). She asked Mash to go with her to Whitt's. He said he would if she insisted; and she did insist (Mash). Deskins proffered to go (Mash), and said he would befriend her (Mrs. Henson). Trent told her he thought she had better not go, as Mr. Henson would be home soon; and if he did not come home in two or three days, that he, (Trent) would be up, and go with her to Whitt's (Mash); but he assigned no other reason to her why she ought not to go (Trent). Presley Davis also advised her to do nothing until Mr. Henson came home. She said she would let it alone, if she thought her husband would be home soon; but that she was afraid Bradley would run away, and she wanted something done first (Presley Davis). She requested Trent, Mash and Deskins, all to go with her (Trent): but Trent excused himself and said something about a shooting match (Mrs. Henson); and that he had to go for bullet-moulds (Trent). Deskins said he would lead Whitt into the light of the affair, and assist him, as he was very illiterate; and Mrs. Henson observed she expected Whitt had not the law-book, as shortly before he had borrowed her husband's—so they took Hening's Justice along (Mrs. Henson).—Mrs. Henson, Deskins, Mash, Trent and Bradley, left the house of Henson about the same time. As Deskins and Bradley parted, Deskins said to Bradley, "if you will befriend me I will befriend you (Mash)." Deskins, Mash and Mrs. Henson proceeded together on foot towards Whitt's, about 200 yards, when Deskins sat down on a log, and said one was enough to go with Mrs. Henson (Mash), and that Mash would have the river to wade (Mrs. Henson); and left it to Mrs. Henson which should go (Mash). She insisted both should go, and never agreed Mash might return; but said, that if only one would go, she would rather it should be Deskins, as he knew most of the affair. Deskins at that time appeared to act reasonably, and was in no wise out of the way (Mash).

Mash returned, and Mrs. Henson proceeded with Deskins, riding behind him on the same horse. They crossed Clinch river at the distance of about four hundred yards from the house of Henson. For about the distance of three hundred yards more there was scarce any path (McGuire); and the way led up a gravelly ridge, the surface of which consisted in some places of nothing but white gravel (Whitt). In passing along where the trace was very dim, Mrs. Henson observed that no body travelled that way: Deskins replied, "Oh yes! madam." Soon after he began some indecent discourse. She requested him to change the subject, as it was disagreeable. He asked her to kiss him. She said she would not. He asked her if she would not give up to him as his own country women did. She said she would die first. *"Well,"* said he, *"here is the ground on which you shall die."* She jumped down and fled, making towards home, as she supposed. She looked round and he was tying his horse. She ran on; but being a very bad runner he was up with her immediately. He seized her wrists in one of his hands, and threw her down. She begged him not to rob her of her chastity; and told him she would give him their negro girl, and all the property her husband owned, if he would let her go. She also told him, that if he would take her home, she would open her door that night, and let him into her bed. She shrieked; and still when she did so, he laid the hand which was disengaged on her mouth, and with the other still kept fast hold of her wrists. He told her that he would keep her there until moon-up. She struggled until her breath and strength were exhausted, and then he accomplished his purpose. He threatened to put her to death unless she promised never to divulge it; and she made the promise. He insisted she should let him into her bed that night; and, under fear, she promised him that she would. He suffered her to rise; and she desired him to let her return home to her little children. He said she must go on to Whitt's; otherwise her return would lead to a discovery, as she lived on the great road. She went on with him; and took up the riding coat and the book which she had dropped in her flight. He desired her to ride; but she alledged she was a bad rider, and afraid; and would not. He snapped the book out of her hand, and carried it. They went on towards Whitt's. A great part of the way was broken and muddy. When they came in sight of Whitt's house, Mrs. Henson told Deskins she would have revenge (Mrs. Henson).

Upon their arrival at Mr. Whitt's, as soon as Mrs. Henson set her foot on the steps, Mrs. Whitt observed that something extraordinary was the matter with her (Mrs. Whitt). Deskins stepped in foremost, handed the book to Whitt, and said they had come to see something about a slander that Bradley had propagated against Mrs. Henson. Mr. Whitt took the book, handed seats, and began to look for the law (Whitt). Mrs. Whitt supposing from the looks of Mrs. Henson something was the matter with some of her family, asked if her family were well. Mrs. Henson replied that they were. She then asked for some water; it was sent for, and brought. She drank, and took out Mrs. Whitt. When they were out of doors, she said, "I put myself under the care of Deskins to fetch me here about that slander of Bradley's; and the wretch has abused me in a shocking way." She then related to Mrs. Whitt the whole story in the same way as on the trial, as near as possible. Mrs. Whitt took Mrs. Henson to be crying; her voice appeared like crying; but Mrs. Whitt did not notice any tears. Mrs. Henson appeared both distress'd and angry. In reply to something said by Mrs. Whitt respecting the danger of Henson's peace being disturb'd, should he hear of what had happened; Mrs. Henson said, she never would lie by her husband's side, until she told him (Mrs. Whitt).

Mrs. Whitt and Mrs. Henson came into the house. Mrs. Henson said to Deskins, "Have you done what you promised me? (Whitt, jun.)." Deskins reply'd, "he's got the book." Whitt said he could not find the law. Mrs. Henson said he need not trouble himself (Whitt). Mr. Whitt looking at Mrs. Henson, and observing that her countenance appeared as if something was the matter, ask'd her if she was sick. She answered, *"It is worse than sickness with me."* Deskins said to Mrs. Henson, "come, let us go" (Mrs. Whitt). She refused to go with him (Whitt), and said Mrs. Whitt had promised her husband should go (Mrs.

Whitt). Deskins ask'd her what was the reason. She said she had put herself under his care, and he had sorely abused her (Whitt). She then ask'd Whitt if there was law for her (Mrs. Whitt). He said there was. She said she would swear the rape. Deskins stepp'd about angrily; dar'd her to swear it; and said he could prove himself clear (Whitt). She replied, *"You wretch you, I will swear it."* Deskins told Mrs. Whitt to take out Mrs. Henson, and search her. Mrs. Whitt said "I shall not search her. I see no outward marks. I see her hands and face, and no marks on them." Mrs. Henson said, *"Yes, you wretch! that's a fine come off. You've abused me at a horrid rate."* Whitt told her he would hear her oath. She hesitated; and ask'd if Major Bowen and Major Ward could not be sent for, and was answered in the negative (Mrs. Whitt). Whitt told her, if she swore it, he would give her a warrant; and as she lived on the great road, she might send it by some careful body to the constable! She then begg'd of Whitt to go home with her, and see her safe to her little children (Whitt). Whitt offered to send for a horse; but she would not wait for one.

Whitt, his wife, Mrs. Henson and Deskins set off together. They went a different road from that Mrs. Henson and Deskins came, in order to cross a large ridge at a lower gap (Whitt). Mrs. Henson appeared in great distress (Mrs. Whitt). Her limbs trembled (Whitt). And Whitt had to assist her over logs that lay in the way (Mrs. Whitt). She appeared far spent and weak. Her distress did not seem so mild as when one has lost a relation; but more insupportable (Whitt). As they went Deskins offered to take Whitt along the way he had brought Mrs. Henson, and show him the whole way. Mrs. Henson said, "If you do it is more than I can." Deskins said he considered her as slandering him; and demanded from Whitt, a writ on the spot. Mrs. Henson appeared alarm'd; and said, *"O pray sir, do not do it!"* Deskins seem'd desirous to talk with her; but she seem'd averse; and he appeared to think hard of it (Whitt). He said to her, "I reckon you want me to give a great deal to make it up;

but I will not give one farthing (Mrs. Whitt)." They had got to
the top of the ridge. Whitt took Mrs. Henson by the arm, attempted to turn her round, and said, "If you incline to compromise, I would bind him;" (meaning to secrecy). She said, "I will
not do it at all;" prevented his attempt to turn her round; and
seem'd angry (Whitt). They came to where the roads parted, at
or near the river, where a canoe was kept. Deskins ask'd Whitt
to stop and talk to him. Whitt did so. Deskins ask'd Whitt if
he thought that Mrs. Henson would swear the rape. Whitt answered that he thought she would. Deskins then ask'd what the
consequence would be? Whitt said, death or the penitentiary.
Deskins then said, "Let her swear it; I'll prove myself clear;" and
rode off. Whitt return'd to his wife and Mrs. Henson. The latter ask'd what Deskins had said. Whitt told her what Deskins
had said (Whitt). According to her testimony, Whitt told her
Deskins said he could prove by three witnesses he never laid
an immodest hand upon her. Mrs. Henson exclaim'd, "O Lord!
is it possible there is a contrivance to ruin me and my family!"
(Mrs. Whitt). Whitt answered, "I really conceive there is some
treachery in it. It looks as if there was a scheme form'd (Mrs.
Whitt)." Mrs. Henson said, "How is it possible he can prove
himself clear, unless some of them went round and watched?"
She then ask'd Whitt what he would advise her to do. He said
he could not advise her. She said, "I do not know what to do.
If I swear it, and he proves himself clear, it will look bad on
my side; and if I conceal it, and it comes to my husband's ears,
it will be terrible.—I am in a dreadful situation." She ask'd if
there was a limited time for commencing such a prosecution.
The answer did not appear. She said, "Suppose I swear it, and
he proves himself clear, what will be the consequence?" Whitt's
answer as he said on the trial, was, "It will represent a bad consequence to yourself." As Mrs. Henson stated his answer, it was,
"If he brings three witnesses to prove himself clear, you will be
put in the pillory." As they approach'd near to the house of Mr.
Henson, Mrs. Henson said to Mr. Whitt, "Do sir, look if there is

any dirt or stain on my back." He look'd and on the lower part of one of her shoulders found a stain about the size of a dollar, of the colour of dry leaves, or soot water (Whitt). He told her that her back was not much dirty (Mrs. Henson).

They came to the house of Henson. Whitt or his wife said they must go home (Mrs. Whitt). Mrs. Henson requested they would stay all night; and said she was afraid Deskins would take her life, as he had threatened it. Whitt told her they could not stay; and that she need not be afraid, as she was in a christian country. She more than once or twice said her life was in danger. She said she had been so hard threatened that she could not but consider herself in danger (Whitt). Whitt desired her to go home with him and his wife, and take her youngest child. She refused. It was a very inclement evening (Mrs. Whitt); and snow'd (McGuire). According to the testimony of Mrs. Henson, Whitt allowed it would be best to send for Deskins. Whitt cannot *form a faith*, whether he proposed sending for Deskins or not; but *thinks* he might. He is confident he did not *actually advise her*; but might say something similar to it (Whitt). Mrs. Henson said to Whitt, "You are the fittingest person to go (Whitt)." Whitt said he would do any thing to pleasure her (Mrs. Whitt); and went for Deskins; whom he found in his own lane. When Deskins came to the house of Henson, he at first would not come into the house. Mrs. Henson said to Whitt, "tell him to come in." He came in; and the following dialogue ensued:

> *Deskins*—What do you want with me?
> *Mrs. Henson*—Concerning this affair.
> *Deskins*—Well what concerning this affair?
> *Mrs. Henson*—You must swear.
> *Deskins*—I'll swear if you'll swear.
> *Mrs. Henson*—I will not swear.
> *Deskins*—Well, I will not swear.
> *Mrs. Henson*—Then let it lie as it is.

Whitt—(to Mrs. H.) I am ready to give you your oath.

Deskins—I am ready to swear I will never divulge it, unless
you, or yours, or the law compels me.

Mrs. Henson—Well, swear.

Upon this Whitt took up the bible, which lay on the table,
and swore Deskins, that he would not divulge the affair, until
Mrs. Henson, or her's, or the law compell'd him (Whitt).

Mrs. Whitt testified that after Deskins had taken the oath,
Mrs. Henson said to him, "I reckon you'll get in your groggy
fits, and tell it yet." Whitt testified he had heard something of
such discourse; but it might be a declaration since that time.
Mrs. Whitt also said Mrs. Henson begg'd the affair might not
go out of their family. Mr. Whitt testified that Mrs. Henson
never ask'd him not tell it, and that he believed it was a proposition of his own; that he said he would order his children not
to mention it. He also testified, that from the situation he saw
Mrs. Henson in, he thought she had Deskins sworn in order to
procure safety; to prevent Deskins injuring her, until she had
the protection of her husband. Mrs. Whitt also testified that
she thought Mrs. Henson's object was to keep Deskins in peace,
until her husband came home.

Deskins, Whitt, and Mrs. Whitt departed.

It was now dark; and Mrs. Henson barr'd up her door (Mrs.
Henson). Presley Davis came there in the night. Before the door
was opened he was ask'd who he was. On telling his name he
was let in, and Mrs. Henson ask'd him to stay all night. He did
so. His residence was one mile distant. Mrs. Henson did not
rise from her chair during the evening. She appear'd mightily
disturbed about something, and in a good deal of distress. She
lay in bed next morning until he went away. Before he departed, she requested him to come and stay the next night (Presley
Davis).

It is proper here to introduce some circumstances which
have not fallen into the narrative. On the morning of the day

on which the rape was committed, three showers had fallen; the last about 10 o'clock, as is supposed from the testimony of Presley Davis; who said he left Henson's about 9 o'clock, and had rode three miles before that shower fell. Deskins and Mrs. Henson got to Whitt's about 12 o'clock, as appeared by the Sun then shining out (Mrs. Whitt). The distance from Henson's to Whitt's is one mile. Mrs. Henson wore a white petticoat, a striped cotton short-gown, a broad shawl, and an every day straw bonnet, tied on her head. Whitt testified that when she came to his house, two streaks of her hair hung down below her bonnet; and that he never saw it off. Mrs. Whitt swore that her bonnet was off; and that her hair lay smooth, and was put up with a comb. She also said that she observed the bonnet was neatly made; and that she did not perceive it to be broken, or her cloaths to be rumpled, or dirty, except her coat about the tail. Deskins appeared to Mrs. Whitt to be sober, as at other times. Mr. Whitt said Deskins did not appear to have been drinking; but he smelt liquor in his breath. Deskins had on a great coat, which he wore all the time he was at Whitt's. Mrs. Whitt swore his overalls were of lindsey; but whether they were *blue* or *pale red,* she could not tell! [*Editor's note:* Lindsey is a coarse fabric.] Mr. Whitt also testified that Deskins is a strong man; and that Mrs. Henson is one of the weakest sort of small women.

On the evening of that day, Trent told his wife (as he confes'd to John Davis) that he expected Deskins would put some questions to Mrs. Henson that would be uncivil (John Davis).

The transaction remained quiet until the evening of Thursday the 16th of January; when David Henson, and his neighbour John Davis, return'd with Henson's waggon from Philadelphia. As they pass'd the house of Deskins he came out, and threw some wood out of the way of the waggon. He walk'd some steps along the road, asking some questions, but keeping at a little distance. When he left them, Davis remarked to Henson that there was something the matter with Deskins (Henson). They arrived at the house of Henson, who met his wife on the floor. On asking her how she was, she said, "I am alive, and as much. They have been ruining of me every way they could." She then commenced telling the story of slander by Bradley, as reported by Mash and Trent. Henson said, "Damn them; you need not regard them, they cannot injure you;" and went out to loose his horses, and return'd. Davis also came in, and having requested Henson to feed *his* horses that night, departed. Mrs. Henson then again spoke to her husband, and said, "will you hear me out?" He sat down; and she told him the whole story of her wrongs by Deskins. Henson arose, and look'd to his gun rack; but there was no gun there. He stepp'd to his shot bag, and drew a butcher knife. Mrs. Henson begg'd him to desist; said that if she lost him, she would be utterly desolate; offered to go on her knees to entreat him; and observed to him also, that as Mrs. Deskins was in a tender situation, he would be the death of more than one. His two eldest children also hung round him. The negro woman lock'd the door, and ran up the stairs with the key. Henson reflected, and resolved to put the law in force (Henson).

On Friday morning Henson went to Whitt's, and applied for a warrant against Deskins. He also requested Whitt to come to his house, and examine Mrs. Henson (Whitt). He proceeded, and collected Mash, Trent, and Bradley, John Brown, and James Brown, another justice. They were all at Henson's on Friday evening. Some one mentioned the suspicion that there was a plot against Mrs. Henson. Mash said he was willing to clear himself on oath (Mash). Henson took out Trent, and ask'd him if he was willing to swear it was not a plot; and if so, desired he would swear; and expressed a wish to get Bradley to swear also. In the night, Mash, Bradley and Trent were sworn by Brown, "that it was not a plot; that they did not know of Deskins going to commit the act; and that they knew nothing to the prejudice of Mrs. Henson." Bradley swore also, that "if he had said what was stated of Mrs. Henson; it was a lie; but that he did not know that he said it (Trent)." Mrs. Henson was examined privily before Brown and Whitt. Her relation of the circumstances attending the rape, was the same in substance as that delivered before the jury, but delivered in fewer words (Whitt). The warrant was then made out, and it was resolved to take Deskins early in the morning.

Accordingly early on Saturday morning, John Brown, Mash, Trent and Bradley, proceeded to the house of Deskins, and arrested him while yet in bed. He arose, and appeared very merry. He told Brown he was his waiting-man, and must go out with him; and when out of doors, he voided his urine on Brown with a loud laugh (Trent). The guard and Deskins proceeded, and met Henson, who advanced with a butcher knife, reproaching Deskins, and seem'd as if he would stab him. The guard took the knife from Henson. Deskins was not tied, and made no attempt to fly. They were then near the top of a steep river cliff. He was brought to Henson's and committed. While at Henson's Trent got Hening's Justice, and read to Deskins the passage in which it is said, rape shall be punished with death (Trent). Henson went on with the guard as they conducted Deskins to the court-house. At Otey's, Deskins called him aside, and offered him his effects, or any part of them only to give him a chance to run. Henson told him that ten miles square on Clinch river would not satisfy him. Deskins wept, and ask'd Henson to have mercy. *"O you villain!"* said Henson, *"why did you not have mercy, when she begg'd you to have mercy and not to rob her of her chastity!["]* (Henson).

On their arrival at the court-house, as the jail was insufficient, it was judged expedient to keep the prisoner under guard in the tavern of William George. His legs were chain'd together with a trace, fastened with two padlocks (Hall). On Saturday evening William Williams examined the laws touching the punishment of rape, both the former and the latter, and read the latter to the prisoner, which provides that the offence shall be punished by confinement to the penitentiary for not less than ten, nor more than twenty one years. Deskins said he thought before, or he knew before, that was the law. Some persons mentioned in his presence, that they would rather die than be confined so long. Deskins said they did not know what they would do until they had the trial. On the same night, Deskins said he would give up all he had to satisfy Henson. Williams told him the case was in the law, and satisfaction could not be taken (Williams).

On Sunday morning a private conference took place between the prisoner, his brother, and the deputy sheriff, behind the corner of the tavern. It was said to the prisoner, that he ought to have escaped before. He requested the deputy sheriff to let him have a chance to escape; and told him he should not lose by it. He offered a particular sum, which the deputy sheriff said was not very large; but the amount of which he cannot recollect (Hall).

Different opinions were expressed by the inhabitants about Tazewell court-house as to the punishment of rape, some contending it was death: But John Grills, formerly a member of the General Assembly, having on Saturday evening or Sunday morning, declared that the punishment was confinement in the penitentiary, and mentioned the year that the act passed, that opinion prevailed (Mrs. George).

On Saturday night, as the deputy sheriff lay on the floor asleep, as he testified, the prisoner took the keys of the padlocks out of his pocket; loos'd the chain from his legs, and sprang against a window, but the sash resisted his force, and he was caught by one of the guard. The deputy sheriff informed him he thought his attempt to escape was evidence of his guilt (Hall).

On Monday at day break a boy of William George's came to William Williams, who resides in the village at Tazewell court-house, and informed him that Deskins desired to see him. He went. Deskins told him he wish'd him to carry a message to his wife, to inform her she need not send for counsel; that he had made an attempt to escape and fail'd; that his case was thereby rendered obvious; and it was useless to employ counsel (Williams); that he thought it better to keep his property for his wife and children (Hall). He said that if he had taken his wife's advice, he never would have come to what he had; that she had often wet his bosom with her tears (Williams). Williams agreed to go for two dollars, the distance being ten miles, and went. Deskins, the same morning after Williams was gone, told Wm. George that he wish'd to see Henson (George). He said he was guilty, and never would deny the fact; that Mrs. Henson was innocent; and would still be esteemed by all good people (Mrs. George). He would submit to her mercy, and go on his bended knees. He would give all he had in the universe to Henson to make it up, and him and his wife, and their children would travel to some place where they were unknown. George told him the case was in the law, and Henson could do nothing for him. He commenced this conversation himself (George). No one ask'd him to confess. No one held out any hope to him. No one threatened him (Hall). He was cool and sober (Williams).

Afterwards, on Monday or Tuesday, some one said that if he was to go to the Penitentiary, it would do no harm to make his will. It was said it would be better to settle his affairs then than after conviction. He refused to make any will (George).

On Wednesday or Thursday in a conversation between the prisoner and Mrs. George, she said she supposed there were some in partnership with him. He ask'd how many. She said she supposed three. Said he, "that's all," or "that's enough;" she cannot tell which. He then said he had to suffer all, and the rest must go clear; but that he would die before he would betray his trust; for it was but to die any how. A Mr. Davis who was present ask'd him something concerning the plot; and Deskins said, "when I started to go, and got as far as my new barn, I wanted to turn back, but they urged me to go on." He said of Trent, Mash and Bradley, who had been named, "keeping such company as that has brought me to what I am (Mrs. George)." Mrs. George being ask'd if it was not difficult to understand Deskins, said, "I know every word he says when he is sober.["] He seemed sober.

On Friday the 24th of January, the examining court was held, and continued on the 25th. Although Deskins had ordered that no counsel should be sent for, yet his wife's father chose to send, and he was defended by counsel. They ask'd Mrs. Henson if she had any marks of violence. She answered that she did not know, that she had not examined; but that she was very sore (Mrs. Walker). The counsel requested some women might be appointed to examine her; and the court appointed Mrs. Walker, Mrs. George, and Mrs. Williams to examine her. The took her into a room, stripped off her dress, and found on the back part of her left arm, above the elbow, a bruise extending over the whole back part of the arm, which was somewhat swelled (Mrs. Walker). It was of a yellowish green color. On the lower part of one of her shoulders was a place that appeared bruised; of the same colour; and also the skin was grain'd, or scratch'd, as if press'd or drawn along gravelly ground (Mrs. George). On the other shoulder was a smaller bruise, of the like colour. One of the women (Mrs. Williams) did not notice it. On one of her arms below the elbow was a slight mark, like the mark of a grip; but the coldness of the day rendered it quickly so indistinct that they did not think it necessary to say any thing of it at the examining court.

The fact of carnal knowledge by Deskins of Mrs. Henson, was admitted by his counsel on the trial. And now the question was, did it take place by her consent or not?

To induce the jury to infer consent, the following evidence was produced:

Aggy Harper—Said that Henson and his wife had quarrelled respecting her being jealous of him; and that Mrs. Henson had told her she never would forgive him as long as she lived.

Molly Harper—Mrs. Henson appeared fretted with Henson; and talk'd of it (her jealousy understood) as lately as last December.

Sally Harper—Mrs. Henson appeared angry a year ago; and told this witness, that Henson had abused her and the family on account of another woman.

James Harper said he heard Henson and his wife talking of it; and she told him she had as good a part in it as he had; (the right to commit adultery understood).

Mrs. Henson was brought into court, and ask'd by the prisoner's counsel, if she had not been jealous of her husband.* [*Quere. Was the decision of the court, that this was a proper question, a lawful one? Can a wife be asked if she does not suspect her husband of a crime?] She answered that she must acknowledge that she had had some jealous thoughts. She was asked if she had not quarrelled with her husband respecting his conduct. She answered that she had talk'd to him concerning it; but not in anger.

Two of those Harpers were examined to another fact.

Aggy Harper said that on the night of the birth of one of Deskins' children, Mrs. Henson and several of the neighbouring women were at the house of Deskins. After the affair was over, Mrs. Henson told Deskins, that if he would go home with her, they would have fine fun on the road!

Molly Harper—They were drinking stew. Mrs. Henson said to Deskins, "If I get drunk, and you go home with me, we'll have fine fun on the road." The witness said it appeared like a joke, that Deskins was talking to other women, that Mrs. Henson drank none at that time that the witness remembers; that she rather supposed Deskins ask'd Mrs. Henson to drink; that Mrs. Henson ask'd this witness to go home with her that night, and she did so.

To destroy the effect of this evidence the counsel for the commonwealth offered to prove, that by the general reputation of the country the Harpers are mulattoes; but that was refused to be admitted by the court. They then introduced witnesses to impeach their credit, to wit:

John Crocket said the Harpers are women of not much respectability, on account of their vices; and one of the men is said not to be a man of truth.

William Cecil—The Harpers are loose shackling people; and there is a talk that they will swear false.

Hezekiah Whitt—The witness James Harper is deranged, and subject to phrenzies. He is not himself at times, and talks a great deal.—Aggy Harper put some goslings in the pasture of this witness to graze. Mrs. Henson and her came there, Mrs. Henson claiming them, and Aggy Harper gave them up. Whitt says the Harpers are industrious.

William Smith—The Harpers are disrespectable. This witness also said he was at the house of Henson an evening about a year ago. There was a talk about Henson and one ———. Mrs. Henson came over the story that night. She appeared to think there was something of it, but spoke of it mildly, and rather laugh'd.

The prisoner's counsel introduced

Mrs. Airnhart—She said that on the third of April last, wanting to borrow a slay, she went to Mr. Henson's for that purpose, and got into a conversation with Mrs. Henson. [*Editor's note:* A slay is part of a loom.] That she told this witness that she would rather Deskins would come home than go to the Penitentiary. That she was sorry she had said any thing about it; and if she had not thought them vile wretches were watching, she would not have told it; that she look'd back and thought she saw Frederick Trent, and knew he was such a vile creature he would tell it. On being cross examined she said, that was the second time she had been at the house of Henson; that Mrs. Henson began the conversation; that it appear'd to the witness she had seen Mrs. Henson at Whitt's; and it appear'd she had seen her on the road near Harper's, the other side of the river. But on being further interrogated, she can't say it was at Whitt's she saw her; nor can she say it was Mrs. Henson she met near Harper's. The reason she recollects so exactly the day of the month, is that on the same evening she was at her uncle's and they were talking over the days of the month. She said that Squire Walker and his wife overtook her on the same day as she came from the house of Deskins.

To destroy the effect of this evidence, the counsel for the commonwealth introduced

Mrs. Henson—She deposed that a woman came to her husband's house, with whom she cannot say that she had any acquaintance; but who had been once there before. The woman began to talk of the misery of this witness, and said, "Pity you had not hallooed until somebody would have heard you." That she (Mrs. H.) had answered that she had hallooed and struggled until she had no more breath or strength to do either. That the woman pretended she wanted to borrow a reed. That she (Mrs. H.) keeps no loom. That she suspected at the time the woman wanted to get something to swear. That Mr. Walker and his wife were there the same day. That she ask'd Mr. Walker and his wife if they saw the woman; and told them she suspected her business; and that she got nothing by coming.

Samuel Walker, says that as himself and his wife went to the house of Mr. Henson about the first of April last, they saw Mrs. Airnhart leave the house of Deskins, going towards the house of Henson; and that they pass'd her. When they came to Henson's, Mrs. Henson said she expected the woman was to be a witness, and had come to pump her. She had had no society with the woman[,] who had been there but once before. That she had asked the loan of a reed and geers [*Editor's note:* equipment for weaving], which she (Mrs. H.) had not to lend, and thought her neighbours knew it. That Mrs. Airnhart asked her why she did not scream and halloo mightily when Deskins attacked her. This witness says Mrs. Henson seem'd intimidated; and said she thought there were people who would betray and injure her; and that she had been cautious of Mrs. Airnhart.

Mrs. Walker, says that when her husband and herself overtook Mrs. Airnhart, her husband observed he supposed she was one of Deskins' favorites. When they came to Mr. Henson's,

Mrs. Henson said she was afraid of the woman, that she had asked her, "Why, madam, did you not scream and halloo, until somebody would have heard you?" That Mrs. Henson related that the woman said she came to borrow a reed and geers; and added, "God knows all my neighbors know I never had such a thing." This witness also says that on the same day she and her husband saw Mrs. Airnhart in company with a sister of Deskins.

Some evidence was produced to impeach the credit of Mrs. Airnhart.

Hezekiah Whitt, said that Mrs. Airnhart is reputed to be a vicious woman. Being ask'd by the prisoner's counsel if that related to her want of truth, or chastity; Mr. Whitt said he thought a *vicious* person, not full of either *truth* or *chastity*. He said that Mrs. Airnhart was never at his house with Mrs. Henson to his knowledge.

William Smith, said the character of Mrs. Airnhart was generally *tolerable bad.*

There was some evidence introduced to prove Henson had malice towards Deskins:

——— *Prichard*—Henson bought some sheep of Smith Deskins. The prisoner would not let him have them, claiming a purchase also. Henson said, "You are a damn'd mean rascal." He also said in speaking of the prisoner, "I'll be up with him. I'll have satisfaction in less than seven years."

John Hankins—After a dispute at town, Henson was saying something of Deskins. Hankins said it was bad for one neighbour to talk so of another. Henson said he would not wish to injure any man; "but they have used me mean, and I'll have satisfaction." This was last year in the summer or fall.

There was some evidence introduced to prove that Henson was of a vindictive temper.

John Hankins—Henson ask'd him if Airnhart's wife was summoned as a witness on this trial. Henson said it was well if some people did not come back with their ears cropped. Henson's enemies speak ill of him.

John Ward—Henson is a spirited spiteful man if insulted. But if he is not insulted, the witness knows no harm of him. He is also tolerable easily offended; and is rather overbearing.

This evidence was opposed by the following:

John Davis—Last fall Henson lent his waggon to Deskins; and when Henson was about to set out for Philadelphia, Deskins promised to do any thing in his power for Mrs. Henson.

David Henson admitted there had been enmity between the prisoner and himself; but said they had become friendly. That he had a quarrel with Smith Deskins last November and some words with the prisoner, who interfered; but a few days after, the prisoner borrowed his waggon and two horses to gather his crop of corn. That Deskins had conveyed him some distance on his journey to Philadelphia; and had promised to bring a bag from mill, or the like, for his wife in his absence.

There was some evidence to prove that Mrs. Henson was not consistent in her relation.

David Ward—Said Mrs. Henson told him the story and related the whole nearly as she related it to the jury, except this; she said to him, that Deskins would sometimes attempt to kiss her; and when she attempted to cry out, would lay his hand on her mouth; and when she turned her head, her mouth was so among the gravel, dirt and leaves, that her cries could not be heard any distance. He said that in every thing else her words bore the same meaning as those she used here. She told him she made all the outcry she could, and struggled until she had no more strength. He was asked if she expressed malice. He said she appeared in a great degree of dejection, mixed with anger and revenge. He was asked if she prevaricated. He said she did not; and that her manner impressed him with confidence in her relation. In answer to some other interrogatories, he said, that she told him she attempted to escape, and looked round, and she either said he was tying his horse, or that she thought he was tying his horse; that she attempted again to escape and immediately he was up with her. That she ran for home; but was always lost in the woods and might have ran another way. That the reason she went on to Whitt's was because Deskins had threatened her life, so she was obliged to go where he pleased. That she was afterwards so sore she could scarcely go about the house, otherwise she would have come to the house of the witness.

William Taylor, was interrogated as to some of the testimony of Mrs. Henson given at the called court. He says he *thinks* she said that "she picked up the book, and gave it up to Deskins." He *thinks* she said she was lost, was the reason she did not go home, but went on to Whitt's.

To counteract this evidence the commonwealth's counsel produced Mrs. Henson's deposition taken before the examining court, in which is this clause; "She then attempted to return home; but he prevented her for fear of being suspected; and this deponent not knowing the locography of the place which the said John had taken her to, and *from compulsion*, was obliged to follow him."

They also examined

Mrs. Walker—She said she had heard Mrs. Henson tell her story five times; twice privately, before the examining court, before the grand jury, and before this court; and that it was uniformly the same in substance, though she might have varied in words. Being interrogated by the prisoner's counsel as to some part of the evidence given by Mrs. Henson before the examining court, she said Mrs. Henson related, that as well as she knew, she ran towards home; but was lost. That when she looked round he was fastening his horse. That when she came to the coat and book, she took up the coat and she supposed the book. That Mrs. Henson being asked the distance from where the fact was committed to where the book and coat lay, said she was not a judge of distances; it was some short distance.

Mrs. George—Said she had heard Mrs. Henson tell her story three time[s]; and that it was the same thing still.

William George—Mrs. Henson at the called court, said she wanted to go home after the fact; but was prevented by Deskins.

Mrs. Williams—Said she had heard Mrs. Henson's relation

of the story three times. That it was always the same in substance, but varied in words.

The prisoner's counsel introduced

——— *Ratliffe*—Who swore he heard Mrs. Henson say that what she had done, or *what she was going to do,** was to retrieve her character; but it seemed as if she was to lose it among them. [**Alluding (as is supposed) to her intention of having Bradley apprehended and examined.*]

Question by prisoner's counsel.—Did she say that *what she swore* was merely to save her character? *Answer.*—No.

Some evidence was given to the character of Trent, Mash and Mrs. Henson, with which this statement shall close.

CHARACTER of TRENT.

James Brown,—Says he is acquainted with Trent. That he drinks and gets into scrapes: But at other times is a *judicious citizen,* and may be depended on.

William Smith.—People are divided as to the character of Trent as a man of truth; some say that he is a man of truth, and some say that he is not. This witness cannot say on which side is the majority.

David Ward.—Trent is considered as an immoral man. This witness knows nothing for or against his character as a man of truth.

John Crockett,—Rather thinks Trent a profligate character; but would prefer that other witnesses should give it, as Trent and himself have had a difference.

Harry Smith—The character of Trent is that of an immoral man, of a profligate, wicked disposition. This witness never heard any thing about him as to truth.*

[**Trent sued a person for charging him with hog-stealing, but dismissed the suit himself.*

Deskins, as he went to the penitentiary, informed Mr. Benjamin Clark, that two others were in Co. with him, and ought to go to the penitentiary as well as himself, but that he would not betray his trust.

Maclin (a fellow convict) told Deskins in presence of the guard, that he hired Trent with bacon to swear for him. Deskins did not deny it; although he denied other things Maclin stated.]

CHARACTER of MASH.

Harry Smith—Says that he has never heard any thing *in favor* of his character as a man of truth. This witness does not *know* that he has heard the credibility of Mash as a witness impeached; but *thinks* he has. His character is that no dependance is to be put on any thing he says, or promises; and if a story comes from *Henry Mash*, it is not minded.

CHARACTER of Mrs. HENSON.

Abner Hall,—Says she is generally accounted a very respectable woman.

Samuel Walker, Resides 12 miles from Mr. Henson's residence, which as well as that of the witness is on the great road. He has made Henson's house a stopping place. He has had an acquaintance with Mrs. Henson for ten years. Never knew her to be a witness. Never heard her credibility impeached until this trial. She has borne the character of a respectable woman, as much so as any lady he knows.

Mrs. Walker—Says she is not very intimate with Mrs. Henson. Has seen her several times; generally at meeting. Has been acquainted with her character. It has been good. This witness never heard a harmful word of her until this began. Has heard Mrs. Henson's character highly spoken of. She has bore the character of a woman of truth.

Mrs. George, says she has known Mrs. Henson for eight or nine years, and that she has sustained the character of a respectable woman, and a woman of truth.

William George says he has been for eight or nine years acquainted with Mrs. Henson; that he always called at Henson's as he passed, and Mrs. Henson was frequently at his house. He never heard any thing against her character until this happened; and never heard any thing but that she was a woman of truth. She has sustained the character of a respectable woman, and been accounted among the most respectable women in Tazewell.

Mrs. Peggy Smith says she has been acquainted with Mrs. Henson for six or seven years. That they have been several times at each other's houses. Mrs. Henson has borne a respectable character, and been considered a woman of truth.

Mrs. Williams, says she never was at Mr. Henson's; she has been acquainted with Mrs. Henson some years, and knew her character two years before she knew her person. She bore a respectable character as far as this witness ever heard, until this affair; and also the character of a woman of truth. Her character was good, and one of the most respectable.

Mrs. Cecil, says she has had an acquaintance for nine or ten years with Mrs. Henson, who bore during that time a respectable character; and the witness never heard her truth impeached.

David Ward, says he has been acquainted with Mrs. Henson ever since she came to Tazewell. He has heard nothing against the respectability of her character; and never heard her veracity doubted. She has sustained actually a respectable character.

John Ward, says he has been tolerably acquainted with Mrs. Henson for some years. That he resides ten miles from the residence of Mr. Henson. Mrs. Henson has borne a respectable character as far as this witness has heard, and that of a woman of truth; he never heard the contrary. She is among the most respectable women in the neighborhood.

John Crockett, says he has been for six years acquainted with Mrs. Henson, and thinks himself pretty well acquainted with her character. Her general character has been good; and this witness never heard any thing against her until this affair.

Hezekiah Harman, says he has been acquainted with Mrs. Henson for some time. She has borne a good character generally, among the most respectable in her part of the country.

William Taylor, says he has a small acquaintance with Mrs.

Henson. He has been perhaps twice at the house of Henson. The general character of Mrs. Henson is respectable.

James Taylor says he has a slight acquaintance with Mrs. Henson. She has borne a respectable character, as far as he has heard.

Thomas Whitten says that for eight or nine years he has had an acquaintance with Mrs. Henson. She actually bore a respectable character. She is one among the most respectable ladies of Tazewell. She never was examined as a witness that he knows of, and he never heard any thing against her truth. She is in the first class of women in our country, from her carriage and conduct.

William Gilmore says he has been acquainted a little with Mrs. Henson. He has been twice at Henson's; but has heard of the family and of their general character 6 or 7 years. Mrs. Henson's character was good until this affair. She ranked among the best kind of women.

Charles Hays, says he has been six times at the house of Mr. Henson. That the general character of Mrs. Henson has been good, as far as he has heard. He has always considered she bore a character among the first rank, as well since this affair as before, among respectable people.

Samuel Ewing says he now resides 40 miles from the residence of Mr. Henson, but formerly resided within about 25 miles. That he has made it a point to lodge there when on business in that part of the country. He has been acquainted with Mrs. Henson for seven years. Her character is good. She is one of the first rate of the women of the country.

John Davis says he has been acquainted with Mrs. Henson eight or nine years. That he never heard any thing of her but the character of a decent modest woman, until this affair, and a woman of truth.

William Smith resides three miles from Henson's. Never heard a disrespectful word of Mrs. Henson, until this affair, only her neighbors say she is above keeping company with the generality of poor folks.

Harry Smith says he has been some little acquainted with Mrs. Henson for seven or eight years. She is esteemed among the respectable women, and seemed to wish to form her acquaintance among such. Her wish to associate only among the most respectable, has created her enmity among the less respectable.

Alexander Cathcart says he has seen the prosecutrix on yesterday, and the preceding day, but not before for ten years. He knew her in Ireland. She lived with a widow relation of her's, a Mrs. Lowndes. The character of the prosecutrix was good. She was on a footing with the best society of the neighborhood; and visited the most respectable houses; among others, that of the clergyman of the congregation. She married while very young. One of the prisoner's counsel asked this gentleman, if she visited *the nobility*. He answered that none of the nobility resided in the neighborhood. The same counsel also asked the witness if the prosecutrix was not *a Roman Catholic*. He answered that for from six to twelve months he had seen her often at the Presbyterian meeting-house, and supposed she was a Presbyterian.

The arguments of the prisoner's counsel were very able; and the delivery of them occupied twelve hours. The heads thereof are given in the following imperfect epitome. [Editor's note: The numbers in parentheses here designate which attorney was making the point. The attorneys and their respective numbers are listed at the end of the summary.]

ONE witness is low proof (2). As chastity is the greatest ornament of the sex, a woman will do any thing to restore herself to the reputation of being chaste. (5). The weakness of the sex ought to be considered (3). Mrs. Henson takes the oath to save her reputation; and is entitled to the less credit, as she did not take it until her husband's return (2). The innocent have been accused of rapes in England (5). Respectable women are sometimes unchaste (5). They have even suffered the embraces of Africans (3), of which our statute book furnishes evidence (6). If a

woman was to go to bed to a man undressed she could not afterwards be believed if she swore he ravished her (3). Mrs. Henson on this occasion went through the woods with the prisoner
alone, which is coming near the supposed case (3). She at another time invited the prisoner, who is a lecherous man, to go
home with her in the night (3). Deskins was allured to the act
(2). She put herself in the way of temptation (3). She imprudently put herself in the power of Deskins; and riding in contact
with him upon the same horse, tended to create incontinent desires (1). Her husband had been from home some time; she was
jealous, and feigned a pretext to go to Whitt's to seek an opportunity (1). She was advised not [to] go then, but chose to go, to
secure the opportunity (1). Bradley had offered a lye-bill, and all
his property; she had therefore no occasion to go to Whitt's (1).
The resistance on the woman's part should be the utmost possible exertion (2). Anger is the antidote to lust; and Mrs. Henson should have bitten Deskins (3). The law of nature is that
the female cannot be forced without being greatly abused (3).
Should two men fight on the ground in a rainy day, the under-
most would be very muddy (4). Mrs. Henson's petticoat was not
dirtied, her bonnet was not broken, and her hair lay perfectly
smoothe (1); they therefore understood each other (5). As one of
the hands of Deskins was occupied holding her wrists, and the
other in covering her mouth when she hallooed, she had but
to halloo to keep both his hands constantly employed, and so
to prevent the rape until this time (1). The fact happened near
a path, where a rape was improbable (2). Had she cryed aloud,
she would have been heard by Mash (2). It is improbable that
Deskins would immediately after committing a rape have tak-
en her to Whitt's, the sanctuary of justice, where she might at
once accuse him (2). The first subject she talked of at Whitt's
was Bradley's slander (2). Her expressions of indignation were
but common (2). Her face was neither bruised nor dirty; and
her agitation was probably feigned (6). Deskins requested she
might be examined, and offered to shew the ground they had

travelled over (6). The marks found on her were probably received at another time (1); and the spot on her short gown was probably produced by a drop from the chimney (1). The witness in a case like this should be consistent; and there are contradictions in the testimony of Mrs. Henson; and she is contradicted by the other witnesses (6). She spoke to the prisoner in a low tone of voice at Whitt's before she complained (2). She accommodated with Deskins (2). [*Editor's note:* "Accommodated with" means "settled with."] She requested the Whitts not to tell the story (2); and would have concealed it but she was afraid Deskins in his groggy moments would divulge it (5). Her fear that she had been watched is a conclusive circumstance against her (1). Deskins had a right to suppose she would tell her husband, as she refused to swear; and had a rape taken place, he would have fled immediately (6). Yet he did not keep out of the way (3). Mrs. Henson was not afraid of Deskins, or she would have went home with Whitt and his wife (6). She is under the influence of Henson, who has deep rooted malice against Deskins (2). She suffered drinking men about her house in her husband's absence (3). She suffered Mash to sit at her bed side, while she lay in bed (1); and was pleased with the obscene exhibition of *the belt* (3). Deskins by hearing the story of *the belt* was encouraged to attempt her chastity (2). The witnesses for the prisoner are decryed because they are poor (6); and those for the commonwealth are selected because they are wealthy (3). Mrs. Airnhart is submitted to God and her country (6). The confession made by the prisoner was made with a view to reconcile Henson to the proposition of an accommodation (1). And Deskins might confess himself guilty of a crime, and not know what constituted it, or what was legal consent (2). There might be some intimidation, or something improper (4); but hope or fear destroy a confession (6); and as to the confession of the plot, although Mrs. George, who proves it, is respectable; yet she was very desirous that Deskins should be punished (6).

1. Mr. Moore,
2. Mr. W. Thomson,
3. Mr. M'Henry,
4. Mr. J. Thompson,
5. Mr. F. Smith,
6. Mr. Sheffey.

The Argument to the Jury

After Mr. Walker, and Mr. Dixon, had spoken in support of the prosecution; and Mr. Moore, Mr. Wm. Thomson, Mr. M'Henry, Mr. J. Thompson, Mr. F. Smith, and Mr. Sheffey, had spoken on behalf of the prisoner; Mr. Smyth addressed the jury as follows:

GENTLEMEN OF THE JURY,

I CAN truly declare that from the first time I appeared at this bar until the present day, I have never risen in any case wherein I was so solemnly impressed with its importance, as I am with the importance of that in which I now address you. It is not to the prisoner and the prosecutrix alone that this cause is important. It deeply concerns the peace and happiness of society.

In performing the duty which I am to discharge, I will endeavor to avoid any address to the feelings. Indeed I find it necessary to do so. I will speak to your reason and your judgment only.—My argument will be necessarily desultory, and without arrangement. The course pursued by those who have gone before me is that which I must follow. I shall be as brief as possible, only taking the time necessary to place the case before you in a perspicuous point of view.

There are various kinds of evidence that may satisfy a jury of the guilt of a prisoner, charged with the commission of a crime. This effect may be produced by either positive proof, concurrent circumstances, or a voluntary confession. When these three different kinds of evidence of the commission of a crime are united, they form the most satisfactory proof of guilt that can be offered to a court and jury.

In the case before you this powerful combination of evidence exists. Here are direct and positive proof of the perpetration of the crime; a chain of concurring circumstances which no ingenuity could fabricate and combine; a voluntary confession of guilt; and added to these, an attempt on the part of the prisoner to fly from justice. This combination is supposed to furnish the most unanswerable, the most irresistible evidence of guilt, that ever was offered in any criminal case in this court. It is indeed supposed that no intelligent man can have heard this evidenc[e], without being thereby convinced of the guilt of the prisoner at the bar; unless his mind is so warped by prejudice, or so poisoned by interest, that he is no longer in a situation rightly to exercise his judgment. It is thought that the disinterested, unbiassed man, who can reject this mass of evidence, is incapable of perceiving and distinguishing truth.

In what criminal case were a positive oath by so respectable a witness; a chain of pregnant circumstances so satisfactory; a confession so ample, and so entirely voluntary; and an attempt by the prisoner to fly, combined together? Certainly not in any one that has ever been tried in this court. Judge Blackstone, speaking of the evidence in the case of rape, has said; "If the witness be of good fame; if she presently discovered the offence, and made search for the offender; if the party accused fled for it; these and the like are concurring circumstances, which give greater probability to her evidence."

Let us compare the testimony of Mrs. Henson with the provisos here laid down. And first let us enquire, "Is she of good fame?"

This question is answered by more than twenty of the most respectable persons residing in the county wherein she dwells, and in the counties immediately adjacent. It has not only been proven that she is respectable; but that she is one among the "most respectable," one of the "first class" of women in our country. She is not only proven to have borne this character for the last ten years; but it has been proven that even in her childhood she was respectable. Her past reputation has been fully sustained. The witness is "of good fame."

It is said the witnesses who support her character have been selected on account of their wealth; and that they ought to have been the near neighbors of the prosecutrix, to whom she is best known. If the selection is an improper one, let the blame attach to the counsel for the commonwealth, by whom it has been made.—Two of the witnesses who support her character reside within three miles of her residence. The rest dispersed through the country all around. It certainly cannot detract from the reputation of the witness that she is known beyond her immediate neighborhood. And if her near neighbors are obscure, what purpose would the production of them answer? If witnesses are called to give the character of a witness, they should themselves possess a character, and it should be known to the jury. The witnesses we produce answer this description. Their respectability is well known to the jury.

One of the counsel for the prisoner was pleased to say that the selection appeared to have been made with a view to national prejudice. The observation has no foundation in fact. It must have proceeded from some mistake; as the gentleman who made it cannot have intended to state any thing but truth. Of upwards of twenty witnesses produced to prove what has been the character of Mrs. Henson for the last ten years, one only is from the country which gave her birth. All the rest are native citizens, as the prisoner is. They cannot have been selected with a view to national prejudice.

A question was asked by one of the prisoner's counsel, that seemed to indicate an opinion that persons professing the Roman Catholic religion ought to be excluded from our courts of justice; or if not rejected as incompetent to be examined as witnesses, that they ought at least to be considered as incredible. According to this doctrine, the women from one half of Europe might be forcibly violated by Americans with complete impunity! Shall we in imitation of those uncharitable and despicable bigots, who would shut heaven's ever open gates against the members of every sect but their own, bar the doors of our courts of justice against all who are not of some favorite religious faith? If any man who hears me entertains such sentiments, my soul abhors him as a tyrant; as a foe to the equal rights of man, who would deprive his fellow men of religious freedom. Shall man presume to prohibit man from rendering in the mode he thinks most proper, worship to his God? What is it to me whether my neighbor prefers his supplication to the highest throne of heaven, or more humbly requests the intercession of mediators, saints, or angels? To all mankind but himself it is certainly indifferent. This question ought not to have been asked in a court of justice in Virginia, where religious freedom rests on the basis of the constitution; and where the law provides that no man's religious opinions shall diminish or enlarge his civil capacity. Whatever may have been the motives that dictated this odious question, it has proved ineffectual. Mrs. Henson appears even in her early youth to have been a Presbyterian. It is therefore presumed that although she is a native of a foreign land, even religious bigots will admit that her person is to be protected, and her testimony heard.

"Is the witness of good fame?" Had we not been able to trace her from an early period of her life; and had she not been known to all the most respectable persons within twenty miles of her residence; yet her conduct throughout relative to this transaction; the various facts which have here been detailed; the testimony that she has given, and five times repeated without any variation; would entitle her to a "fair fame." She appears to unite simplicity with innocence; faithful chastity with a degree of gentleness that the counsel on the other side seemed to suppose could not exist. To prove her unchaste by inference, the court have suffered them to ask her if she was not jealous of her husband; as if the incontinence of a husband, who regardless of the value of the jewel in his bosom seeks after strangers, ought to subject the injured wife to foul suspicion. The question has been asked, and it has been answered. She has acknowledged that she had entertained jealous thoughts of her husband; and has said that she has talked to him concerning his conduct; but without anger. This the counsel on the other side cannot believe: But to me it appears agreeable to the general gentleness of the female character; and consistent with the most perfect female art.—It is true there are among women some who would meet an unfaithful husband with frowns, and load him with reproaches. The counsel are mistaken who suppose this the character of all the sex. There are others who would endeavor, like Mrs. Henson, to reclaim lost affection by blandishments and smiles. There are others who, like the unhappy wife of the prisoner at the bar, would water a faithless husband's bosom with their nightly tears.

Some wretches have testified that Mrs. Henson had spoken malignantly of her husband; that she had vowed never to forgive him as long as she should live. Fortunately a respectable witness, whose testimony is unimpeached, has heard a conversation between Mrs. Henson and her husband on the subject of his infidelity. She spoke to him in such a manner as proves the mildness of her temper; the goodness of her disposition. It seems to me impossible to see her, and hear her relate the story of her wrongs; and not feel attachment to her cause and sympathy for her sorrow tremble in every nerve. Yet amiable as is her disposition, fair as is her reputation, she has been assailed by calumny: But the dirt that has been cast against her, has recoiled upon the heads of those by whom it was thrown.

We will not rest this case on the general reputation of Mrs. Henson, and her positive oath that the crime has been committed; although she is of good fame. We will trace her through all the circumstances attending this fatal transaction. Let us commence on that morning when the base instruments of seduction, the panders of a ruffian's lust, the conspirators against virtue, the supposed accessories to rape, informed her of the story the half ideot Bradley had been induced to tell, to the injury of her character. She felt that uneasiness and indignation such information might be expected to produce; and which it was probably intended to produce. Bradley on the following day, as it is said, offered a lye-bill, and all his property, by way of satisfaction. She is censured for not accepting this satisfaction. But to one who has been slandered, and who is conscious of innocence, the receipt of compensation would be less satisfactory than an investigation. To obtain an investigation appears to have been Mrs. Henson's desire. The proper means of obtaining it appear to have been to her unknown.

On Tuesday Deskins and his co-conspirators came again to the residence of Mrs. Henson.—She had heard of Bradley's slander before; but as Trent and Deskins on that day told her the whole, and advised her how to proceed, that seemed to be their business, as she perceived no other. She has therefore said "they came to tell her." She listened to their propositions, and determined to follow the advice given by Deskins and Trent, to have Bradley apprehended. Trent, with the art of a practised pimp, in order to place her alone in the power of Deskins, told her he could not then accompany her to the house of a magistrate, but that he would on some future day; informing her at the same time that Bradley was expected to leave the country immediately. This determined her to go at once to a justice. She declared she would not then go, were it not that she feared Bradley would leave the country. Deskins perfidiously proffered his friendship. Deskins who once indeed had a slight difference with her husband, but which then was settled; who had been appointed to assist her in any difficulties that might occur;—a man possessing some knowledge, and pretending to more, he offered his services. She agreed to go with him, insisting that Mash should also go. The three together set off for Whitt's. A scheme was suggested for sending her on with one only of those men. She never consented to the arrangement: But her reputation being dear; and her journey as she was taught to believe necessary to its salvation; Deskins being a neighbor, the most respectable man, and the best informed; she preferred him to accompany her. The woman who is conscious of virtue does not apprehend that every man with whom she is alone will solicit her chastity; and she knows that should the shameless attempt be made, she can indignantly repel it.

It has been said that Mrs. Henson "went to Whitt's without a cause, to secure *an opportunity*." The evidence does not authorise such a conclusion. *Mash* says, "She asked him to go; he promised he would if she insisted; and she did insist." He also says "Deskins' advice and Trent's, was to have Bradley taken." *Trent* says, "She seemed anxious to go to Whitt's, and asked them *all* to go along with her." He says also that "She said Deskins was accustomed to the law; and she seemed to choose he should go along; Mash was to go with them." *Davis* says, "She told him she would not go, but that she was afraid Bradley would run away, and wanted something done first." This evidence proves, that anxious to preserve a reputation that was dear to her, she wished the slanderer apprehended. She would willingly have put it off until the time of her husband's return; but Bradley was about to leave the country. She asked all three of them to go with her; and insisted on Mash to go, and Trent said he could not. She was indeed advised, *not to go;* but never advised, not to go *with Deskins*. She would have followed the advise: But an apprehension that Bradley would leave the country precipitated her into the unfortunate plan of going to Whitt's with Mash and Deskins.

Mrs. Henson could not have set out with both Deskins and Mash, "*to secure an opportunity*." Let us see by whose contrivance it was that Mash left them, and returned. *Mash* says, "Deskins sat down on a log, and said one was enough to go with Mrs. Henson. She insisted both should go. She never candidly gave up for him to go home." It is plain the proposal that one only should go on with her; came from Deskins. He indeed said that Mash might take his horse and go with Mrs. Henson; but that proposal he knew would probably be rejected. It would detain and give trouble to Mash; and the ignorance of that man, would render abortive the visit of Mrs. Henson to the house of the justice.—Deskins probably expected that Mash and Mrs. Henson would both object to the proposal, and so it happened. The proposal was artfully made; it tended to get Mrs. Henson in his possession alone, by preventing any suspicion on her part of his design.

But that Mrs. Henson was desirous to be with Deskins alone, is a position unwarranted by any proof. The very reverse is proven; yet it does not appear that her endeavor to retain Mash in company with Deskins and herself, proceeded from any doubt of the honor of Deskins; but from a wish to have Mash before Whitt as a witness.

That Mrs. Henson did not desire to be alone with Deskins, seems to me to be clearly proven. Let us then presume that Deskins had no preconceived improper design, and that without design on either side, they were in the woods alone. Does it excuse a man in a case like this; that the woman was in the woods alone with him? Can he plead that "he was allured to the act?" Then every rape will be excusable, for none are committed publickly, or without temptation.

It is said that "She imprudently put herself in the power of Deskins." Is it then criminal not to think Deskins the most abandoned of the human race? I agree it was an error; but the unsuspicious disposition of Mrs. Henson, ought not to devote her to utter destruction. And shall the accused be suffered to say in a case like this "She trusted me, therefore I am excusable in betraying and destroying her?" No. Never until confidence shall become a crime. Never until treachery shall become a virtue. Shall the perfidious traitor alledge his violation of the most sacred duties; his violation of a confidence reposed in his honor and his protection, as an excuse for the vilest guilt? If so the host may murder his sleeping guest, or rob him of his treasures, and say, "Why did he trust me?" The guardian may ruin the ward who has chosen him, and say, "Why did she trust me?" The false and perfidious friend may betray and ravish his neighbor's wife, and say, "Why did she trust me?" If so, let all confidence be banished from among mankind; and let suspicion, the villain's virtue take its place.

The consideration that Mrs. Henson had put herself in the power of Deskins, instead of being an argument to excuse him, adds a thousand fold to the atrocity of his offence. Had he met her accidentally, and ravished her he would have deserved death; but for thus abusing her, when she had put herself in his power, under an idea that he was a friend—he deserves damnation.

This unsuspicious woman having put herself under the protection of Deskins alone, after they had crossed the river, as they were passing through the woods on a gravelly hill, before they had reached the road leading to Whitt's, he solicited her chastity.

No act of the prosecutrix can please the counsel of the prisoner. They say she should have fled from Deskins on the first indecent solicitation: But an attempt to ravish does not uniformly follow an attempt to seduce. She had a right to suppose that a decided refusal would put an end to his solicitations. Must she always attribute to Deskins principles constituting the extreme of villainy?

She found indeed that there was not any act of villainy too atrocious for Deskins to commit. From this woman thus situated can man expect more than she has done? Formed on a most delicate model; as weak as gentle; can we expect from her, against a man remarkably muscular and strong, an effectual resistance? She declares she will die before she will yield her honor. She flies. She struggles until her shoulders and arms are bruised and lacerated; her breath and strength exhausted; until every nerve remains trembling, and every limb incapable of performing its office. But I hasten from this scene, where treachery triumphed over confidence, and brutal lust was sated with the spoils of violated chastity. A scene most afflicting to every friend of virtue.

It is objected to her that she did not, upon the perpetration of the act, immediately return home: But has she not been threatened with death? Has she not under fear promised to admit the ravisher to her husband's bed? Shall she refuse to comply with his further mandates, when the refusal cannot restore to her what she has lost? What is so likely to qualify a ruffian to commit murder as having committed or attempted a rape? Who has not read the story of Jason Fairbanks, and Betsy Fales? Who does not know that within a few years past, there have been several women murdered, after having been ravished? Had not Mrs. Henson a right to fear, that Deskins, having gratified his desires, would, if she discovered a design to prosecute, secure his safety by her death? Yes; she had a right to fear. Yet she exhibited all the resolution we could have expected. She refused to ride with him; and as soon as she saw the house of Whitt, she declared her determination to have revenge.

She "presently discovered the offence."

It is objected to the evidence of Mrs. Henson, that she is contradicted by other witnesses, and that there are contradictions in her own testimony. That there are any contradictions in her testimony, or between it and that of other witnesses, that ought in any manner to discredit her evidence, I deny. The lynx-eyed counsel may discover what is imperceptible to common sight; but let us attend to truth and common sense. Mrs. Walker, a lady of excellent understanding, declares she has heard Mrs. Henson repeat her story five times, and that she has never varied in fact, although she may have varied in words.

As to some of the alledged variances between the testimony of Mrs. Henson and that of the Whitts, whom I admit to be well inclined people, they are wholly immaterial. Whether the one or the other is correct makes no difference, where the fact is unimportant. Whether Mrs. Henson did or did not expect her husband *soon,* (a term which may mean five minutes or a month); whether the day was "somewhat cloudy" or "a rainy day;" whether Deskins "jumped about in a passion;" or "stepped about angrily with odd turns;" are enquiries quite trivial, and unworthy of observation.

But the Whitts contradict each other materially. Thus Whitt says that Mrs. Henson, before she went out with Mrs. Whitt, spoke to Deskins, in answer to which he said, "he has got the book." Young Whitt proves clearly it was after she had been out with his mother, that Mrs. Henson spoke to Deskins, and received that answer. Mrs. Whitt says that Mrs. Henson had her bonnet off; her hair lay smoothe; and was put up with a comb. Whitt says that two streaks of her hair hung down below her bonnet; and he never saw it off. Mrs. Whitt supposes that the proposal to send for Deskins was made by Mrs. Henson. Whitt thinks he might have made the proposal himself. Mrs. Whitt says, Mrs. Henson begged that the transaction might not be mentioned out of their family. Whitt thinks *that* proposal was his own: that he said he would order his children not to speak of what had happened; and he says she never asked him to conceal it. In exhibiting the contradictions among these people, who are witnesses as well for the commonwealth as for the prisoner, I mean not to detract from their credit. They probably each of them intend to speak truth, and come as near to it as they possibly can. Their contradictions are to be ascribed to the imperfection of all human testimony, which must, from its nature, be fallible. I only desire, that as you will not, for material variances, condemn the testimony of any of the Whitts; so neither will you, for immaterial variances, condemn the testimony of Mrs. Henson.

There is indeed one part of the testimony of Mrs. Henson, which is to be preferred to that of Mr. Whitt. It is that which regards the advice given by him to Mrs. Henson, not to swear the rape until she should be further advised, and to compromise with Deskins. To give counsel, Mr. Whitt now perhaps considers improper and contrary to his duty. To advise an injured party to compound and conceal a felony, is, in a magistrate, a serious crime. Whitt is not bound to prove he committed it.

And when he denies this, he swears for his own exoneration; and is, as to that fact, far less credible than Mrs. Henson.

That Whitt did discourage Mrs. Henson from immediately swearing the rape, appears probable. He himself proves that he indirectly proposed a compromise. This is agreeable to the character of Whitt; who is a man attached to peace and quiet, and of an easy disposition.

It has been said the fear of Mrs. Henson that they had been watched, is a circumstance which proves her guilt. I understand this part of the evidence in a different manner. Mrs. Henson observing a private conversation between the justice and Deskins, anxiously enquired what Deskins had said. In the testimony given by her and Mr. Whitt, the answer she received is stated somewhat differently. Whitt says Deskins had said, "Let her swear the rape; I will prove myself clear;" and that this he reported to Mrs. Henson. But she says Whitt informed her that Deskins had said, "he could prove by *three witnesses* that he never laid an immodest hand upon her." Mrs. Whitt has told us that Deskins had utterly denied having carnal knowledge of Mrs. Henson. Here then was no intimation that Deskins would attempt to prove her an adulteress; but a threat to prove her perjured; in as much as he denied carnal knowledge of her, and said he could prove himself clear. She concludes that there is a conspiracy to ruin her, and acquit Deskins by perjury; that Trent, Mash and Bradley, might have been near the road, and that they will swear, "Deskins did not lay an immodest hand upon her." She exclaims, "Is it possible there is a conspiracy to ruin me and my family?" Whitt supposed there was some treachery, and a scheme to effect her ruin. She considers that without a conspiracy, that unless those associates were sent round to be near the place, they cannot presume to give any testimony, true or false; and she asks the question by way of argument to prove that a conspiracy must have been formed. "How is it possible he can prove himself clear, unless *they* went round and watched." The question was natural in her situation. She presumed there existed a conspiracy; she expected the production of perjured testimony; and that those who were to deliver it had, that they might be witnesses, went round and watched. They on the other side understand this expression of Mrs. Henson as if she had said, "How can they truly swear he is clear, unless they went round and watched?" But it is not reasonable to presume that she meant to admit she was guilty. We understand it as if she had said, "How can they *falsely* swear he is clear, unless they went round and watched?" Watching, she considered essential to enable them to state plausibly, though falsely what happened. She believed Deskins could prove what he threatened. She knew it would be false; and therefore inferred there was a conspiracy. It cannot be denied that this was, on the part of Deskins a threat to defend himself, and destroy the testimony of Mrs. Henson, by perjury. He threatened to prove what he has not been able to suborn witnesses to prove. Why make such a threat if he was innocent? This threat to defend himself by perjury, was made by him to intimidate the injured, and is persuasive proof of his guilt.

The manner in which Mrs. Henson braved this threat to destroy her reputation by perjury, is an evidence of her innocence. Had she been guilty, knowing that Mash, Trent and Bradley were in the neighborhood; that they were the associates of Deskins; and having therefore grounds to apprehend the perjured testimony would be produced; would she have firmly refused to swear concealment? Or would she not have compromised with Deskins, as it has been erroneously said she did? Would she have informed her husband the first moment she beheld him of the injury she had suffered? Would she have consented to send for a justice to receive her examination before she knew what those associates of Deskins would swear? No. It was a consciousness of innocence that directed the course she pursued. A consciousness that truth was on her side, and that perjury could only appear against her. This it was that enabled her to refuse to swear concealment. It was this decided her not to hesitate one moment, to make the afflicting disclosure to her husband on his return. Had it not been for this consciousness of innocence, she would readily have agreed to conceal the transaction. She would have endeavored to throw over it an impenetrable veil.

It has been said Mrs. Henson would have concealed the transaction, had she not been apprehensive that Deskins, when intoxicated, would reveal it. And the testimony of Mrs. Whitt is relied on; who says Mrs. Henson observed to Deskins, that "she supposed he would get in his groggy fits and tell it." Mrs. Whitt's testimony is not satisfactory to me that this expression was made by Mrs. Henson. Whitt says "he heard something of such discourse, but that it might be a declaration since that time." Whitt would, we must presume, support the testimony of his wife, if he was not strongly impressed with a belief that she is incorrect. He does not confirm her testimony in this respect. He therefore believes her to be incorrect. Mrs. Whitt is probably honest; but you cannot have failed to notice that she unites the worst of memories to an understanding of the weakest grade. It is probable some one has alledged in presence of Mrs. Whitt, that Mrs. Henson was afraid Deskins would reveal the transaction in his groggy moments; and the imperfect understanding and memory of Mrs. Whitt, may have led her to ascribe this declaration to Mrs. Henson.

Had this expression actually been made by Mrs. Henson, Whitt and his wife must have understood her to be desirous of a lasting concealment of the transaction: But they both say they conceived her object was merely to keep Deskins quiet until her husband should return. Then this expression cannot have been made by Mrs. Henson.

Gentlemen of the jury; In this case, *that* has happened which was to be expected. Whenever a rape is committed, it may be expected that the friends of the accused will exert themselves to disparage, traduce and villify the character of the woman who is injured. It is the only mode of proceeding that affords a hope of acquittal to the accused. If the character of the prosecutrix remains unimpeached, the conviction of the defendant is almost certain. His friends will anxiously strive to save him from punishment, and his connexions from that dishonor which his conviction will cast on them, though innocent, by destroying the credit of the principal witness.

The prisoner being possessed of a considerable estate which is liberally expended for his defence, no effort has been left untried to effect his escape from punishment. The talents of six gentlemen of the bar have been engaged. They are indeed a lawful subject of sale and purchase. Attempts have been made to bribe the prosecutor and to corrupt the public officers. Diligent search has been made for witnesses. They have been found. The dregs of mankind have been collected. Persons whom no society, no *colour* will acknowledge, have been summoned. The testimony of some of them shall now be the subject of animadversion.

A profligate vicious woman has been produced to sully the character of Mrs. Henson, and to exhibit her to view, as an adulteress by her own acknowledgment. She swears that Mrs. Henson began a conversation with her, and said, "She had rather Deskins would come home than go to the Penitentiary; that she was sorry she said any thing about the affair; that she would not have done so, only she thought the vile wretches were watching; that she looked back and thought she saw Frederic Trent; and knew he was such a vile creature he would tell it."

It must be agreed that if Mrs. Henson made this precious confession, what she was afraid Trent would tell of, was not *a rape*. This woman had seen and spoken to Mrs. Henson at her own house once before as is admitted. She swore she also saw her at Whitt's; but reflecting that the contrary could be proven, she afterwards said that she could not be certain that she saw her there. She swore she saw Mrs. Henson on the road near

Harper's; and again said she was not certain it was her she saw there. Thus it appears that this woman did not know Mrs. Henson's person. She is proven to be a base character; and Mrs. Henson is proven to be one possessed of pride, who disdains the society of the base. Yet by the testimony of this woman, Mrs. Henson is stated to have confessed herself guilty of adultery, and consequently of perjury, to one of whom she knew nothing, except that she was abandoned and infamous. What must be thought of a defence thus bolstered up by testimony which all mankind must consider false?

The testimony of Mrs. Airnhart contains internal evidence of its falsehood; which is also more fully proved by the testimony of Mr. and Mrs. Walker. On the very day on which Mrs. Airnhart pretends to have received this extraordinary confession, Mrs. Henson declared she had considered her as a spy, who desired to get something to swear; that she had been cautious of her, and told her nothing, only, in reply to an impertinent observation, that she had cried out, and struggled, as much as was in her power.—And on the same day Mrs. Airnhart was seen at the house of Deskins, and in private conference with his sister. These circumstances render it highly probable that this abandoned woman is suborned; that she has shared in the distribution of that estate, which is devoted to procure, by any means whatever, the escape of the prisoner from the punishment due to his crime.

Every action and expression of Mrs. Henson, that seemed to justify an inference that she might be influenced by incontinent desires, have been enquired into, and given in evidence.* How honorable is this investigation to her, when thereby it appears, that her most unguarded actions and expressions, indicate the innocence and purity of her mind.

[*The court decided that the prisoner's counsel were at liberty to prove any particular act of lewdness done by Mrs. Henson to induce the jury to infer consent. A witness (John Ward) was ask'd if he knew any lewdness of her, of his own knowledge.

QUERE

"It is a general rule that a witness shall not be asked any question the answering to which might oblige him to accuse himself of a crime; and that his credit is to be impeached only by general accounts of his character and reputation, and not by proofs of particular crimes, against which he cannot be presumed prepared to defend himself."

2 Bac. Abr. 296.] [*Editor's note:* The quote is from Matthew Bacon, *A New Abridgment of the Law.*]

The wife of Deskins became indisposed, and sent for her female friends. In collecting them, Deskins called on Mrs. Henson, and took her with him a part of the way towards his house, "she riding in contact with him, on the same horse." Conscious of the respect due to her character, she did not apprehend any improper solicitations. The labors of the night being over, the warm beverage circulated, and full cups crowned the birthnight feast. In the midst of all this mirth, when every gossip was lively,* Mrs. Henson was solicited by Deskins to drink. She declined complying with his solicitations, and jocosely said, "If I was to get drunk, and you was to go home with me, we should have fine fun on the road." Two women who were present have given mutilated statements of this conversation. According to *Aggy Harper,* Mrs. Henson said to Deskins, "If you will go home with me, we will have fun on the way." This is proving too much. There is not a prostitute in this district who would thus solicit the chastity of a married man, in presence of his wife, and all her female neighbors. The testimony is incredible; it is contrary to all manner of experience; and not to be believed. You will notice that this witness is the woman who took the young geese of Mrs. Henson, and secreted them in Whitt's distant pasture, beyond a mountain from the river, and gave them up on their being discovered and claimed. She now revenges herself on Mrs. Henson, for reclaiming her property that had been stolen, by giving odious, partial, and malicious evidence.

[*When skirlin weanies see the light,*

Thou make the gossips clatter bright.
       BURNS' ADDRESS TO SCOTCH DRINK.]
    The same conversation has been stated by *Molly Harper* as follows: Mrs. Henson said to Deskins, "If I get drunk, and you go home with me, we'll have fun on the road." This is half the truth. But this witness also said that nobody was speaking to Mrs. Henson; and that Deskins was talking to other women. This cannot be true. It cannot be believed that Mrs. Henson would begin a conversation with such an expression. The witness indeed said again, she thought Deskins asked Mrs. Henson to drink. And if so, and this expression was made by Mrs. Henson as an excuse for not complying with his solicitations, although it is not remarkable for delicacy or refinement, yet it is agreeable to the innocent simplicity, and conscious virtue of Mrs. Henson, and the hilarity of the occasion. But it is to be observed that before the *fun* spoken of was to happen, two other circumstances must happen: First, Mrs. Henson must get drunk; and secondly, Deskins must go home with her. She took care that neither of those circumstances should happen. She drank nothing; and probably was the only perfectly sober person present. For want of a more respectable companion, she took home with her Molly Harper.
    An attempt has been made to prove that Mrs. Henson is destitute of delicacy. *Freder[i]ck Trent* has been suffered to relate for that purpose a story the most odious that ever polluted the ears of a court of justice. But Trent's testimony does not deserve belief. A good man cannot have acted as he says he did; and if he is a villain no regard should be paid to what he swears. He is proven by *Major Ward, Captain Harry Smith,* and *Capt. John Crockett,* to be a wicked, profligate, abandoned, and immoral man. Can you give such a man your confidence? Can you believe a man who proves himself to be a base licentious ruffian, who could, in the grossest manner, insult a respectable woman in her own house, when unprotected and alone? No. You will place no reliance on the oath of a wretch, who disgrac-

es the character of civilized man.—If there is in our country a man utterly destitute of decency, honor, and virtue, Trent is he.

One of the counsel for the prisoner has said, that "If the ruthless hand of a villain had done such an act as Trent performed in the house of a modest woman, she would have ordered him out of doors." You must reflect that Mrs. Henson was alone among inebriated *semi*-savages; and whatever they might do, she dared not to offend them.

But to what does this odious story amount? As it was told by Trent three or four days after the transaction took place, it was merely this—An indecent action was done in her presence—The instant she saw it, she ran out of the room, and did not, during the evening, return. When Trent related this fact to young Brown, he did not know he was to be a witness, to exculpate the man to whose crime he is probably an accessory. He spoke the truth, having no motive to relate a falsehood.

That Trent was deeply engaged in the plan to ruin Mrs. Henson, appears by another part of his own testimony. One of the diabolical crew was to attempt her chastity that night; and two others, of whom Trent was one, were to be spectators of his success. The wretch who was to be the principal in this attempt, shrunk from his undertaking. To avoid it, he got drunk, and went to sleep. A conspiracy against Mrs. Henson evidently existed. She was so unfortunate as to appear desirable to these abandoned men. Her delicacy was to be tried. She was to be seduced if possible. If that could not be effected, she was to be violated by force. At any rate she was to be ruined.

It has been urged as a proof of Mrs. Henson's want of delicacy, that she suffered a man to sit by her bed side while she lay in bed. The gentleman is, I conceive, over nice in this respect. In many a house that is the abode of unsuspected chastity, the males and females lodge in the same room. It would be a hard decision, to reduce a woman otherwise esteemed, to the rank of prostitutes, because a man sat beside her bed before she arose in the morning.

And if the gentleman had succeeded in proving that Mrs. Henson was not remarkable for female delicacy, I should deny that an inference of her want of chastity could therefrom justly be drawn. Delicacy and chastity are by no means inseparable companions. Inflexible chastity is sometimes found associated with indelicate manners; and refined and delicate behavior sometimes accompanies easy virtue.

Gentlemen of the jury—I am persuaded you will divest yourselves of every impression relative to this cause, that may have been made on your minds before you took your seats within these walls. That you will fix your attention on the evidence now given; judge upon that evidence; and upon that alone. The cause calls for strict impartiality, and great deliberation. The question to be decided is serious in its nature; and the decision to be given must prove important in its consequences. Your verdict is necessarily to ruin one of two persons. You must find the prisoner guilty of the crime of rape, and consign him to the penitentiary for at least ten years, or else must fix on Mrs. Henson the character of a lewd woman, and a perjured witness. You cannot but feel anxious to render a verdict consistent with justice.

If on a fair, full and candid consideration of the evidence, you shall be of opinion that Mrs. Henson, lewdly desiring to have criminal conversation with Deskins, went with him from her home for that purpose, willingly submitted to his embraces, and then resolved falsely to accuse him of a rape; that in pursuance of this cruel resolution, she made the accusation; but changing her determination, proposed to conceal the act; that she had the art to initiate the grief, indignation, terror and agitation, that the actual commission of the crime on a woman of sensibility would produce; that to give color to her accusation, she bruised and lacerated her arms and shoulders, but concealed the bruises until they became green, when they were discovered by the management of the prisoner's counsel; I say if you draw these conclusions from the evidence, it is your duty to acquit the prisoner. But you must believe Mrs. Henson to possess a mind more artful, a disposition more cruel, and principles more abandoned than ever yet actuated the worst of woman kind. You must conceive her to be a monster of lewdness, cruelty, falsehood and cunning unequalled by any character recorded in the page of history. You must conceive her to be animated by such a soul as the infernal regions do not yet contain.

If on the contrary, it shall appear to you that Deskins, desiring to possess Mrs. Henson, in order to effect his purpose formed a plan to get her alone and in his power; that the plan proved effectual; and that being unable to seduce her, he accomplished his purpose by force; then your verdict will be that the prisoner is guilty.

That Deskins formed a plan to get Mrs. Henson alone in his power, I conceive is fully proven. An attempt to seduce, uniformly precedes the perpetration of rape. No savage ever violated chastity by force, without first endeavoring to procure the consent of the object of his desires. Bradley, Trent and Mash* were probably privy to the plan, and engaged to aid it. It is probable that Bradley was induced to slander Mrs. Henson, for the express purpose of getting her to leave her home. To distress her was a measure likely to cause her to repose confidence in a pretended friend. That Trent knew the design of Deskins, appears by his having told his wife on the evening of the day of the rape, that he expected Deskins would make an attempt on the chastity of Mrs. Henson. That Bradley was privy to that design appears by the observation Deskins made to him a moment before he set out with Mrs. Henson to Whitt's; "If you will befriend me, I will befriend you." The knowledge of Mash may be suspected, from his first promising Mrs. Henson to accompany her to Whitt's, and then leaving her, without her consent, on the proposal of Deskins. These circumstances combined, must prove a conspiracy, to the satisfaction of the most incredulous mind. [*The expression of Deskins to Mrs. George, "It is

hard that one should have to suffer for three;" and his informa-
tion to B. Clark, that there were two others who ought to go to the
penitentiary as well as himself, lead to a belief that he had only
two confederates.]

And if Deskins did not design to get Mrs. Henson in his
power, why offer to accompany her to Whitt's when she is, as it
is said, the wife of his enemy? Why did he contrive that Mash,
who was going along willingly, and who was a necessary witness, should return, and leave him and Mrs. Henson in the
woods alone? His intention in all this is plain and obvious. To
effect his diabolical purpose, to gratify at once his lust and vengeance, he formed a plan sufficient to impose on an innocent,
unsuspicious woman, who prized her reputation and dreaded
to lose it. The danger of losing the confidence of her husband
was represented to her with infernal art. The deceived woman first trusted herself with Deskins and Mash. Deskins being
thus possessed of his victim, Mash was dismissed; and then the
accomplishment of the object with so much pains pursued, the
gratification of the desires of this monster, by force and violence, followed.

To prove that Deskins accomplished his purpose by force
and violence, we have the express and positive oath of Mrs.
Henson. An oath wherein she relates such incidents and conversation as appear probable; and to invent which would re-
quire an uncommon capacity. An oath by which she could gain
nothing, but what she has already acquired, humiliation, insult, obloquy and disgrace. An oath which it is most improbable she would have taken, had she consented. In that case she
would unquestionably have assiduously concealed the act. But
as it is urged that the testimony of one witness is low proof, let
us consider the attending circumstances, as made to appear by
the testimony of others, that we may be enabled to determine
whether they are such, as might be expected to attend a rape;
or whether they are such as might be expected to follow had the
act taken place by mutual consent.

When Mrs. Henson came to the house of Whitt, she was walking, and Deskins was riding alone. The part of the road nearest to Whitt's is level, and then was very muddy. Why did she walk along this muddy part of the way? Had her consent been granted to the act that had been committed, we might expect that the friendship between her and Deskins would not have been lessened, but much encreased. Her refusal to ride with him again, is a circumstance leading to a belief that he had abused her.

It has been said that Mrs. Henson spoke to Deskins in a low voice at Whitt's, before she revealed the injury she had suffered. The testimony of old Mr. Whitt states her to have done so; but he did not hear what she said; and that he is mistaken, seems obvious from the testimony of young Whitt, who heard the expression, and says explicitly, that it was after his mother and Mrs. Henson had been together out of doors. The only words Mrs. Henson spoke before she revealed the injury was to tell Mrs. Whitt that her family were well, and to ask for some water. She took out Mrs. Whitt, to whom as a woman she could most freely make the disclosure; and weeping with indignation, said, "I put myself under the care of Deskins to bring me here, about that slander of Bradley's; and the wretch has abused me in a shocking way." If she had yielded her consent to the solicitations of Deskins, what subsequent act of his could have caused her to make against him so serious, so cruel an accusation?

It has been said by one gentleman, that "her expressions of indignation were but common;" and by another that "she cried without tears." She has not it seems grieved according to the tastes of the gentlemen. She has not wrung her hands nor tore her hair; nor have her tears flowed incessantly. But although she neither wrung her hands nor tore her hair, her grief appears to have been great. Mr. Whitt has said it was not so mild as that occasioned by a relation's death, but more insupportable. As to tears, they might fall unnoticed; or the exhausted sufferer might have no more to shed. Her countenance evinced the greatest mental distress. It was noticed by Mrs. Whitt the moment she first saw her. It was noticed by Whitt before he heard her complain. The one supposed some of her family were sick. The other supposed she was sick herself. It has been said, "her agitation was probably feigned." But to me that seems to be impossible. The words and actions of distress may be imitated; but the look of agony, the agitation of real distress, as discovered in the countenance of Mrs. Henson, must have been produced by an indignant sense of the degradation she had suffered; of the great, the irreparable injury she has sustained. This appearance could not have been assumed by Mrs. Henson, had she not been injured; nor by the most accomplished theatrical performer. She was either an injured innocent woman; or else she was an adulteress. If she was injured, the appearance of extreme distress was natural; but if she was an adulteress, it was not. Therefore the appearance of distress discovered in the countenance of Mrs. Henson, is powerful evidence of her innocence.

It has been said that "Mrs. Henson was not afraid of Deskins." But the testimony proves that she discovered a great degree of fear. She begged Whitt and his wife to go home, and to stay all night with her. She said that she had been so hard threatened that she could not but conceive herself to be in danger. Presley Davis was not suffered to enter her door that night, until he first told his name, and she was certain that it was not Deskins who desired admittance. The fears she discovered impress the mind with a belief that she had been abused, and threatened as she testifies; and corroborate other circumstances in proving that she was injured.

Proof of those circumstances which usually attend a fact, furnish a ground to presume the fact itself. A circumstance which must usually attend rape, is such a degree of violence as to bruise the female ravished. Marks of bruises, the effect of violence may be expected to appear on the body and limbs of a prosecutrix, after the commission of a rape with force. When a base intention to extort money, or to procure revenge for some insult, produces a false accusation of the crime of rape, it is possible for the false accuser to shew bruises, caused on purpose to be exhibited as evidence. In that case she may be expected to make an immediate and frequent display of them.

Bruises have been found on Mrs. Henson. But they were not displayed by her; although she had complained of soreness. The prisoner's counsel at the examining court, probably expecting that as she had shewed no marks, there were none upon her, required that she should be stripped and examined. It was done as they requested. She was found to be bruised on her back at the shoulders; and on the back part of one of her arms, above the elbow; exactly on those parts where she would be bruised by being thrown down, pressed on the ground, held, and ravished in the manner related in her testimony.—These bruises were seen on the 25th of January, and appeared green and yellow, as if received some time before. The rape was committed on the 14th of January. Thus the appearance of these bruises correspond with the time, and their situation with the occasion on which, as we say, they were received. And they were not displayed by the prosecutrix, but discovered at the request of the prisoner's counsel. Strong presumptive evidence indeed of the injury of which Mrs. Henson complains.

It is contended that more considerable marks of violence ought to appear on the person of Mrs. Henson; and that marks of her resistance ought to appear on Deskins. To this I answer, the bruise on the back part of her arm would probably be occasioned by jerking it against the ground, in attempting to free her hands. Her struggles would necessarily bruise her shoulders as she lay on a bed of gravel, only overspread with leaves. But the strength of Deskins, the diminutive size, and personal imbecility of Mrs. Henson; the manner in which he held her, both her wrists being grasped in one of his hands, and his weight upon her; put it in his power easily to restrain her exertions. [*Editor's note:* In the nineteenth century, the word *imbecility* often meant "want of strength, weakness."] We cannot therefore

expect any marks of resistance on him, nor any more considerable marks of violence on her, than those that did appear. And
I think when it is considered that this feeble, fearful woman
was alone, in a lonely place, with the prisoner, whom she found
to be a wretch unrestrained by any law, divine or human, she
would be excused for not attempting to do him any injury, even
if she had possessed the power. Had her strength been much
greater, and he had failed to accomplish his purpose, or had she
not promised concealment, it is extremely probable she would
have been murdered like the unfortunate Betsy Fales; and Deskins who now stands at the bar as a ravisher, would have stood
there as a murd[e]rer. At one time I conceive he had fully resolved to destroy her. At Whitt's, after she had told him she
would have revenge; after she had revealed the injury to Mrs.
Whitt; after she had told Whitt her disorder was worse than
sickness; Deskins had the audacity to insist she should go home
in company with *him*. He then intended to murder her.

It is said, "her bonnet was not broken, her cheeks were not
bruised, her hair was not dishevelled, and her petticoat was
neither rumpled nor dirtied." Her bonnet was an every day
straw bonnet. It was tied on her head, and might not be injured; and would defend her cheeks from being bruised; and
her hair from being much dishevelled. Two parcels of her hair
hung down below her bonnet, although Mrs. Whitt has sworn
it lay smooth. That her petticoat was not rumpled or dirtied, it
is difficult to believe, when we reflect that she had, on a rainy
day, rode behind Deskins in this petticoat; and that it is contended she prostituted herself to him on that day. That her petticoat was not much soiled, is no more an evidence that she was
not thrown down and held by Deskins, than it is that she was
not down at all; but that is not alledged. The reason her short
gown escaped being dirtied, appears by the testimony. She wore
a large shawl; and the place where the crime was perpetrated
is on a hill, consisting in some places of gravel, unmixed with
earth; and that gravel was then covered with leaves. That Mrs.

Henson supposed her clothes were dirtied, appears by her request to Whitt to look at her back; and that supposition of her's
proves she had been in a situation which she thought likely to
dirty her clothes. A stain of the colour of dry leaves was discovered on her short gown, immediately over the situation of one
of the bruises. It proves she had been so violently pressed to the
gravelly ground, that the dead leaves, which covered the gravel, softened by the showers, were mashed, and communicated
their color to her clothing. It was then her shoulder, immediately under that stain, was bruised and lacerated in the manner described by Mrs. George. Thus the appearance discovered
on her clothing, though inconsiderable, strongly corroborates
the other circumstances, in proving that Deskins succeeded by
force and violence.

It is urged that she sent for Deskins, and accommodated the
matter with him. This is advanced and insisted on as a proof
that she was not really ravished. You will observe the motives
Mrs. Henson had for dissimulation. She had perceived the ti-
midity, indecision, and incapacity of Whitt; and had requested
that Major Ward and Major Bowen might be sent for, on whose
protection and judgment she could reply; and it had been refused. She had enquired how Deskins would be apprehended;
and was told a warrant would be given to her, and she might
send it to the constable. She entreated Whitt and his wife to
see her home, and they did so. She entreated them to stay all
night with her, and they refused. She had been threatened with
death by Deskins if she disclosed the act; and she had disclosed
it. Whitt reluctantly admits he might have proposed to send for
Deskins. Mrs. Henson being under fear of death, and denied
protection by a man whose mind is too feeble for the execution
of an office of authority; who for the sake of quiet would rather hide than punish a crime; allowed Whitt, on his proposal,
to go for Deskins, in order to lull him into quiet and security.
But even then she refused to swear, and did not even promise
concealment. She never promised not to prosecute. She had de-

clared that she would never lie by her husband until she told him what had happened, and she kept her word. Is it a crime in this weak, timid, distressed and unprotected woman, to have endeavored to avert the threatened destruction impending over her, and which she apprehended would be inflicted by a cruel barbarian? I cannot think so. Had she, under the influence of fear, from the threats of Deskins to burn up her and her family, unbarred her door, and let him into her bed, each embrace would have been but another rape. Surely then that fear will excuse the sending for Deskins, with a view to lull him to security; to soften him, and avert his vengeance.

If we reflect on the situation of Mrs. Henson, we shall find that it is difficult to imagine one of greater distress. A weak, lonely woman; ravished by an inhuman monster, and threatened with death. Her husband distant far; and the day of his return unknown. Denied protection by a timid, ignorant man; who though clothed with authority as a minister of justice, is destitute of one spark of that amiable valor which protects society; who suffers the felon to assume command in his house, fears to apprehend him, and proposes to place a warrant against him in the hands of the helpless sufferer; discourages her from prosecuting; and only more and more excites her fears. If under these circumstances she had sworn to conceal the crime, Deskins would not have stood excused thereby. The rape was committed; and his guilt was complete. The injured party could not, by any subsequent consent, excuse it.

Had Mrs. Henson carried farther the plan of concealment; had she even attempted to hide the act entirely from the world, I should hold her absolved from censure. Has not a female thus injured powerful motives for concealment? Is she not by the act, degraded and disgraced? Will her husband, if she is married, meet her again with the same satisfaction? Or if she is single, will she marry to equal advantage? No. Her honor is violated. Her person is polluted, although her mind is innocent. In my esteem a woman thus injured, would suffer nothing by concealing the injury, if, when it should be otherwise disclosed, there appeared satisfactory evidence that her chastity had been forcibly violated. Indeed Mrs. Henson had the strongest motives for concealment. 'Tis not wonderful that for a moment she might hesitate what course to pursue and exclaim, that she was in a dreadful situation. To her, under all circumstances, a prosecution against Deskins must have had peculiar terrors. She was threatened that she should be proven guilty of perjury. She was threatened that she should be murdered. And she risqued her happiness on her credibility. To her, the native of a distant land, whose husband is her only friend, the consequence of losing his confidence would be fatal. This she must have perceived might happen, should Deskins produce the perjured witnesses whom he threatened to produce. The consequence might be her expulsion from the bosom of her family; to wander forlorn; lost to every hope of returning happiness; and infinitely wretched.

To the gentlemen who now impeach Mrs. Henson's fame, I presume it would have been perfectly satisfactory, if after having made the disclosure at Whitt's, and after exhibiting extreme distress there, she had struck a dagger through her heart, and now reposed in the tomb. But let me ask those gentlemen if the material evidence would not have stood then just as it does now? The relation she gave at Whitt's, and the symptoms of distress she exhibited there, are the material evidence. Shall we, because she is not a Lucretia, but prefers life and the society of her family, to fame, and the silent grave, deny her our esteem and confidence? [*Editor's note:* Lucretia was a legendary Roman victim of sexual assault who committed suicide.] Shall we, because love to her husband and her darling children, chains her soul to earth, traduce her as false and meretricious? Forbid it justice! Here is the truly honorable female character. A faithful, patient and affectionate wife; a tender mother; a timid woman. Such is the female character we should cherish and protect.

Among the different arguments used against this prosecution, one is, that it is founded in malice. From whose malice can

it proceed? Is it from the malice of Mrs. Henson? When gentlemen tell you that she invited the caresses of Deskins at his own
house; and that "she went with him to Whitt's to seek an opportunity;" can they tell you also that she prosecutes him from
malice? Can a woman have malice against the man whom she
desires, and who has but complied with her wishes? Can Mrs.
Henson now through malice, prosecute a man, whom the prisoner's counsel say she did not wish to prosecute at all? These
arguments, like the brothers, who sprung from the teeth of the
Theban Serpent, mutually destroy each other. [*Editor's note:* In
the classical story of the beginnings of Thebes, Cadmus plants
the teeth of a serpent he kills. Warriors spring up from the
teeth and fight each other, with the survivors helping found
the city.] Perhaps it is supposed the prosecution proceeds from
the malice of Henson. It has been said he has deep-rooted malice against Deskins. Can it be believed that Mr. Henson, a respectable man, would place his wife in such a situation as Mrs.
Henson has been placed in, exposed to the grin of ridicule, and
the finger of scorn, to gratify malice without just cause? If there
is any one who can believe that Henson would thus sacrifice
his wife's fame and feelings, let him recollect that Mrs. Henson
herself commenced the prosecution before her husband's return. "That fellow," said she to a magistrate, "has ravished and
ruined me. Is there no law for me?" The magistrate pointed out
difficulties; recommended concealment; and defeated the prosecution for a time. It is said the innocent have been accused of
rapes in England; and that Joseph was falsely accused of old.
But I call on the gentlemen from their stores of knowledge, an-
cient and modern, to produce a case where a woman, gratified
in her lawless desires, has sought revenge against the object of
them. Groundless prosecutions for the crime of rape, committed, or attempted, are sometimes commenced, by wretches destitute of character and of feelings. Sometimes the object may
be to obtain revenge. More frequently it is to extort money. Mr.
Henson has not commenced this prosecution as the means of

extortion. You have seen him deliver his testimony, and of that you must be assured. There is not one trait of meanness in his manly countenance. He has been offered the whole estate of the prisoner, which pays to six lawyers enormous fees, and brings here a motley tribe of witnesses. He rejected the offer with disdain. Money, powerful as it is; although it can quiet a lawyer's conscience, when it would reproach him for obstructing that justice an injured woman asks in tears; yet it cannot heal the wounded feelings of a man of honor. Mr. Henson asks indeed for vengeance. He asks it as an injured man; not on a false accusation. The prosecution cannot proceed from the malice of Henson. It cannot proceed from the malice of his wife. It cannot be an unfounded malicious prosecution.

To establish the point, that there was malice between Henson and Deskins, an attempt has been made to prove that Deskins was prosecuted for one crime, his brother for another, and that Henson countenanced the prosecutions. When a good man is unfortunately neighbor to a bad one, or frequently comes in contact with him, hatred is apt to arise between them. But shall the existence of this hatred so operate, that if the villain ravishes his neighbor's wife, or burns his house and family therein, that the good man cannot sustain against him a prosecution? Shall the existence of previous malice be a ground of defence for the criminal? It is a strange defence indeed. I do admit there was malice between these men. I am willing to admit that Henson countenanced those prosecutions; and that Deskins, notwithstanding his pretended reconciliation, still sought for revenge. When barbarians enter an enemy's country, ravishment of the women is one mode by which they execute vengeance. Deskins, being a barbarian, resolved on the ravishment of Mrs. Henson, as one mode of being revenged. For that purpose he formed the plan already spoken of. He insidiously, with infernal art, pretended friendship. She heard him; believed him; trusted herself in his power; and was undone.

Gentlemen, I will now make a few observations on the confession made by Deskins. The other evidence did not leave the case doubtful. But if it had, his confession renders the proof of his guilt conclusive and complete. This confession was made freely and voluntarily. Neither promises nor threats were made to draw it from him. Under these circumstances, it is evidence to be left to a jury, and it has been left to you. It is said to be weak evidence. A confession never can be regarded as weak evidence if there is any corroborating proof. If there is no concurring circumstance, it may be regarded as insufficient evidence. As if a horse is stolen; a month afterwards a stranger is apprehended, and confesses he stole the horse; if he was never seen in possession of the property, and there is not a single circumstance to corroborate his confession; it is insufficient evidence. But where there are corroborating circumstances, a free and voluntary confession is strong and powerful evidence. As in this case; when we consider the obvious plan, the opportunity, the complaint and distress of Mrs. Henson, the bruises, her positive oath, an attempt by the prisoner to fly from justice; when to these is superadded the prisoner's voluntary confession of his guilt; the whole forms a mass of evidence, conclusive, and irresistible.

It is said to be the law, that if a confession is made under the influence of hope or fear, it is to be disregarded by the jury. I understand the law to be, that if the confession be obtained by promises or threats, it is to be rejected by the court. We can have nothing to do with the hopes or fears which the prisoner's own imagination may create. If they have been excited by promises or threats, the court will reject the confession; lest under these circumstances the prisoner may have done himself injustice. In what case a confession ought to be given in evidence, or suppressed, is a question of law, to be decided by the court; and it has been decided that this confession is evidence. If a belief that the prisoner entertained some hopes, or fears, should induce a jury to disregard a confession, every confession would be disregarded; as every prisoner either hopes to be acquitted, or fears to be convicted; but those hopes or fears which he himself creates, can hav[e] no operation. The confession of Deskins has been admitted to be proven, and declared evidence to be weighed by you. It was made in a manner that frees it from all objection, and entitles it to the highest credit. It was produced by the stings of contrition and remorse: and made in a moment when the prisoner was actuated by a virtuous resolution, to meet the punishment he had deserved, and to preserve to his unfortunate family his property, for their support. He has since determined to reduce them to beggary, under a fallacious hope of acquittal. He had not then seen the difficulties which the ingenuity of counsel can throw in the way of innocent simplicity. He had not considered that the depravity of human nature furnished hope that he might procure witnesses to cloud the most spotless character, or render suspicious the purest chastity. He then did Mrs. Henson complete justice. He acknowledged her innocence and his own guilt. I must again say that the unprejudiced and disinterested mind that is not convinced by this evidence, must be dead to the impressions of truth.

Gentlemen,—Having now gone through the evidence in this case, and answered, in a disultory manner, the principal arguments urged on behalf of the prisoner, I will come to a conclusion. Suffer me to remind you that it is not Mrs. Henson alone who is interested in procuring the conviction of the prisoner at the bar. This prosecution is interesting to every woman in our country. If Mrs. Henson does not in this case obtain redress, no woman, hereafter injured in the like manner, can expect redress. If the evidence produced in this case is not sufficient to prove a rape, satisfactory evidence of a rape cannot be given. Thus it will appear that in a society composed of men "whose hearts are resolved and whose hands are ready" to guard the rights they themselves enjoy, protection is denied to the most estimable half of the human race. It will appear that our women may be ravished by monsters, without any hope of being avenged, except by the arm of an incensed husband, a brother, or a father.

Reflect, fellow-citizens, that you are trying the cause of an injured WOMAN; of one of those to whom we are indebted for our being, our civilization, and whatever portion we possess of happiness; of one of those whom we are especially bound to protect, because they are unable to protect themselves. We have deprived them of liberty and property; let us at least maintain them in the right of personal security. If we shall suffer this helpless sex to be violated at will, by the *centaurs* among us, we are unworthy of the character of civilized men.

Should your verdict be an acquittal on this full and clear evidence of guilt, will any injured woman hereafter attempt a prosecution? Will she encounter the insulting looks, impertinent interrogations, abuse, and obloquy, that Mrs. Henson has borne? Will she encounter the perjured testimony of every blasted villain and abandoned prostitute who ever entered her door? No. Far better would it be to suffer in silence the forced pollution of every ruffian she meets, than undertake such a prosecution as this, if such a prosecution as this is, shall prove ineffectual.

Should you acquit this prisoner upon the evidence that has been given, and a woman should hereafter complain of the like injury to a husband, who considers that she is entitled to his protection, and who is ready to sacrifice his life in her defence, what will be his conduct? Will he bring her here to undergo the fiery ordeal Mrs. Henson has experienced? No. A reflection on the denial of justice to one of the most respectable women in our country, will teach him the folly of bringing her here. Every manly feeling of his heart will revolt at the idea. But will the ravisher therefore go unpunished? No. The steel of the injured husband must drink the monster's blood. He will prefer standing behind this bar as a criminal, to seeing his wife stand before it, a disregarded, insulted witness. He will see that it is the only course he can consistently with his wife's honor pursue.

Thus you will take upon you an awful responsibility for every rape, and consequent murder, that the precedent you shall have set may produce. Rapes will be committed; and justice being denied, they will be concealed by the sufferers. The cruel ravishers will at some distant day boast of their victories. And then if the doubly injured women have friends, assassinations will follow. But if "according to the evidence," you find the prisoner guilty; confidence in the protection granted by the laws to the feeble, will encrease. It will be seen that money cannot, by corruption, save a criminal from the punishment due to his crime.

Some gentlemen* [*Mr. M'Henry and Mr. Moore] who appear for the prisoner, have thought proper to declare that they would not appear for him, if they did not believe that he is innocent. They perhaps intend that the weight of their characters shall influence your decision. They are men of truth; and when they make even this declaration, I believe them. Such declarations ought, I conceive, to be omitted. I wish not to express an opinion in any such case, although I might expect to obtain an equal degree of credit, as I stand here, not under the influence of money, to defeat justice; but to assert the cause of injured virtue, and to maintain the violated laws. But this I will declare. If you now acquit this prisoner, I should think myself sinning against society to rise hereafter at this bar, to prosecute a man who had slaughtered one manifestly guilty of ravishing his wife, his sister or his daughter. No. I never will abuse my weak capacity so far as to aid in murdering according to law, the avenger of the violated honor of a woman whom the laws will not protect. If you acquit the prisoner, and an injured husband shall hereafter imbrue his hands in the blood of the ravisher of his wife, when he shall stand arraigned at this bar for that offence, I shall not appear against him.

The Sentencing

VIRGINIA:

At a superior court continued and held at Washington court-house on Friday the 9th day of May, 1806.

The jurors empannelled on Monday last for the trial of John Deskins, husbandman, from the county of Tazewell, indicted for a rape, were brought into court by the Sheriff of Washington county, and having heard the evidence upon their oaths do say that the said John Deskins is guilty in manner and form as in the indictment against him, is alledged, and they do decide upon and ascertain the term of his confinement in the Jail and Penitentiary house to ten years. And thereupon he was remanded to jail.

And at a superior court continued and held at Washington court-house on Tuesday the 13th day of May, 1806.

John Deskins, of the county of Tazewell, husbandman, who stands convicted of felony, was again led to the bar in custody of the keeper of the district jail, and thereupon it being demanded of him, if any thing further he had or knew to say, why the court now here should not proceed to pronounce sentence against him pursuant to law. He said he had nothing further to say, but what he had before said.

His honor Judge Holmes then proceeded to pass sentence upon the said John Deskins, in the following words:

John Deskins—You have been arraigned, tried and found guilty of the abominable crime called rape. Although there is perhaps no society, however polished its manners, or refined its humanity, which can boast of a complete absence of crime; yet, to the honor of our country, it may with truth be said, this crime of which you are convicted, but rarely occurs. And I trust in God we may never again be presented with an example of its commission, under such afflicting circumstances as your case affords. It is far indeed from being an ordinary case. There is in it an assemblage of vices of the most horrid aspect. Base perfidy; criminal adultery; planting a dagger in the breast of the friend of your bosom; all attend the ravishment of your neighbor's wife. Would to God the atonement which you are about to make to your country for the violation of its law, could also heal the wounds of those who have fallen sacrifices to your lawless lust. The same act alike dishonored your own and your neighbor's wife: But if between these victims there was a difference as to the degree of dishonor, the punishment which awaits the act seems to preponderate the scale against the former, so as to balance injuries. This circumstance no doubt has had its effect upon the jury who decided on your imprisonment. They have dealt to you all the mercy which the law and their oaths would possibly admit of. Indeed from the affecting scenes which your trial and its consequences have produced, it was to be feared that the cause of public justice, although asserted by injured virtue, might be melted down in the crucible of humanity. The jury however have taught their feelings to be subservient to their judgment; and having condemned you to an imprisonment for ten years, it now becomes my duty to say what portion of that time you shall spend in solitude, and privation of ordinary comfort. The court therefore directs and appoints, that you be confined in the Jail and Penitentiary house ten years; and in the solitary cells thereof, to be fed on low and coarse diet, for one fifth part of the said time of ten years. Here an opportunity will be afforded you of reflecting on your past life; and although deprived of the light of day, your conscience will prove a faithful mirror to exhibit to your view the agonizing attitudes of a distracted wife, an helpless and dishonored offspring. Here too you will be startled in your slumbers by the shrieks and cries of violated chastity. That the admonitions resulting from these internal evidences of wrong, may prove more faithful to their purpose, than the tears of your tender and affectionate wife, which you acknowledge to have bathed your bosom on former occasions, is my sincere wish.

THE END

Appendix A

"Rape," A section from The New Virginia Justice (1795), edited by William Waller Hening

Key to authorities cited:

Inst.: Edward Coke, *Institutes of the Laws of England* . . . (first published in four parts beginning in 1628)

Dalt.: Michael Dalton, *The Countrey Justice* . . . (first published 1618)

H. H.: Matthew Hale, *Pleas of the Crown* . . . (first published 1678)

Haw. or *Hawk.:* William Hawkins, *A Treatise of the Pleas of the Crown* . . . (first published 1716)

I. What it is.

RAPE is an offence in having unlawful and carnal knowledge of a woman by force and against her will. But it is said that no assault upon a woman in order to ravish her, however shameless and outrageous it may be, if it proceed not to some degree of penetration, and also of emission, can amount to a rape; however it is said that emission is *prima facie,* an evidence of penetration. 1 *Hawk.* 169.

The offence of rape is no way mitigated by shewing that the woman at last yielded to the violence, if such her consent was forced for fear of death, or of duress. 1 *Haw.* 108.

Also, it is not a sufficient excuse in the ravisher, to prove that the woman is a common strumpet; for she is still under the protection of the law, and may not be forced. 1 *Haw.* 108.

Nor is it any excuse that she consented after the fact. 1 *Haw.* 108.

It is said by Mr. Dalton, that if a woman, at the time of the supposed rape do conceive with child by the supposed ravisher, this is no rape, for (he says) a woman cannot conceive except she doth consent, and this he hath from Stamford and Britton, and Finch. *Dalt. c.* 160. [*Editor's note:* Hening here refers to legal authorities William Staunford (1509–1558, sometimes spelled "Stamford") and Henry Finch (d. 1625). *Britton,* a very early book on English law, is often attributed to John le Breton (d. 1275).]

But Mr. Hawkins observes, that this opinion seems very questionable; not only because the previous violence is no way extenuated by such a subsequent consent, but also because if it were necessary to shew, that the woman did not conceive, the offender could not be tried till such time as it might appear whether she did or not, and likewise because the philosophy of this notion may be very well doubted of. 1 *Haw.* 108.

And L. Hale says, this opinion in Dalton seems to be no law. 1 H. H. 731. [*Editor's note:* "L. Hale" refers to Sir Matthew Hale (1609–1676), lord chief justice of England.]

II. Evidence on an indictment of rape.

The party ravished may give evidence on oath and is in law a competent witness; but the credibility of her testimony, and how far forth she is to be believed must be left to the jury, and is more or less credible, according to the circumstances of fact that concur in that testimony. 1 H. H. 633.

For instance, if the witness be of good fame; if she presently discovered the offence, and made pursuit after the offender; shewed circumstances and signs of the injury, whereof many are of that nature, that only women are the most proper examiners and inspectors; if the place, wherein the fact was done, was remote from people, inhabitants, or passengers; if the offender fled for it: these, and the like, are concur[r]ing evidences to give greater probability to her testimony, when proved by others as well as herself. 1 H. H. 633.

But on the other side, if she concealed the injury for any considerable time, after she had opportunity to complain; if the place where the fact was supposed to be committed, were near to inhabitants or common recourse or passage of passengers, and she make no outcry when the fact was supposed to be done, when and where it is probable she might be heard by others; or if a man prove himself to be in another place, or in other company, at the time she charges him with the fact; or if she is wrong in the description of the place, or swears the fact was done in a place where it was impossible the man could have access to her at that time, as if the room was locked up, and the key in the custody of another person: these and the like circumstances carry a strong presumption that her testimony is false or feigned. 1 H. H. 633. . . .

Upon the whole; rape, it is true, is a most detestable crime, and therefore ought severely and impartially to be punished with death; but it must be remembered, that it is an accusation easily to be made, and hard to be proved, and harder to be defended by the party accused, tho' never so innocent: Therefore a wise jury will be cautious upon trials of offences of this nature, that they be not so much transported with indignation at the heinousness of the offence, as to be over hastily carried to the conviction of the person accused thereof, by the confident testimony sometimes of malicious and false witnesses. 1 H. H. 635, 636.

III. Punishment of rape.

Of old time rape was felony, for which the offender was to suffer death: afterwards the offence was made lesser, and the punishment changed from death to the loss of those members whereby he offended; that is to say, it was changed to castration and loss of his eyes, unless she that was ravished, before judgment, demanded him for her husband. 2 *Inst.* 180. [*Editor's note:* The rape victim could demand that the rapist marry her, and he would thus avoid punishment.]

But by *Virginia laws* page 256. "If any man do ravish a woman married, maid, or other, where she did not consent before nor after; or shall ravish a woman married, maid, or other, with force, altho' she consent after, the person so offending shall be adjudged a felon, and shall suffer death as in case of felony, without the benefit of clergy." [*Editor's note:* The benefit of clergy was a policy by which a court could allow the defendant in a capital case one opportunity to avoid execution, but the defendant's thumb would be burned to make clear that the benefit could not be used again. It was a way to mitigate the use of executions if justices saw fit. See Kathryn Preyer, "Crime, the Criminal Law, and Reform in Post-revolutionary Virginia," *Law and History Review* 1 (Spring 1983): 54 n. 6.] "If any person shall unlawfully and carnally know and abuse any woman child, under the age of ten years, every such unlawful, and carnal knowledge, shall be felony, and the offender being duly convicted thereof, shall suffer as a felon, without benefit of clergy." § 2. [*Editor's note:* Even as late as 1885, the age of consent remained at age ten in the majority of states in the United States. See Mary E. Odem, *Delinquent Daughters: Protecting and Policing Adolescent Female Sexuality in the United States, 1885–1920* (Chapel Hill: University of North Carolina Press, 1995), 14–15.]

IV. Principal and accessory.

Mr. Hawkins says, all who are present and actually assist a man to commit a rape, may be indicted as principal offenders, whether they be men or women. 1 *Haw.* 108.

And, so one woman may be a principal to the ravishment of another.

So also may a man be guilty of a rape on his own wife; as was the case of lord *Audley*, who held his wife while his servant, by his command, ravished her. [*Editor's note:* Mervyn Touchet (1593–1631), an English nobleman sometimes known as Lord Audley, was executed in England in 1631 in this famous case involving both rape and sodomy.]

Appendix B

The Trial of Jason Fairbanks (1801)

Selection from *Report of the Trial of Jason Fairbanks, on an Indictment for the Murder of Miss Elizabeth Fales. At the Supreme Court, Holden at Dedham, in the County of Norfolk, on Thursday the 6th, and Friday the 7th Days of August, 1801,* 3rd ed. (Boston: Russell and Cutler, 1801), 7–9.

In opening the trial, the Attorney General stated the importance of the issue, and gave from authorities the definition of the crime of *Murder,* and of what is meant by *Malice aforethought,* which is necessary to constitute the crime and which distinguishes it from every species of homicide. He then stated, that the facts which he expected to maintain the Indictment upon, were, that the prisoner was a native of Dedham; that he was about twenty-one years of age; that, some time ago, he lost the strength and the use of the elbow of his right arm, by inoculation for the small pox, the shoulder and wrist remaining well; that, from this circumstance, he had been kept at school more than labouring lads commonly are, but had lived an indulged and idle life; that he had a kind of fondness for, or rather a propensity towards the deceased in particular, who was the daughter of a respectable family in the neighbourhood, and who was of the age of eighteen years. That on an idea of his not being allowed to visit her at her father's house, they had met elsewhere sometimes; and that though there was no evidence, that she had a wish to marry him, in his present situation, yet that she was attentive to him, and more so than to any other person.

That he was however jealous of others, and had threatened revenge against her parents, on account of a supposed prohibition to visit her. That on Saturday the 16th of May, he had informed two persons, that she and he were to meet in the pasture on Monday, being the 18th, in which he would settle the affair; and that she should consent to go off to Wrentham and marry him, or he would violate her chastity.

This kind of threat[e]ning he had used before; but afterwards had seemed to relent, saying that it would be wrong to ruin her character, for the purpose of having revenge on her parents. That on Sunday the 17th, he induced a young woman to write and sign, with the name of the Town Clerk, a paper purporting to be a certificate of his having been duly published to Elizabeth Fales. That after he had it in his possession, he said, "*Ah!* BETSEY FALES, *this will do.*"

That he told one man, on Monday morning, that he was going to Mason's pasture to meet her, for the purpose above expressed. He had before engaged a horse and chaise to go to Wrentham that week. After one o'clock, the same man saw him on his way to the pasture, and conversed with him again on the subject; and the prisoner informed him, that he would return to him in an hour, and let him know the event. He inquired of him, if he knew, whether any person was going to work near the place that afternoon. On his way he met William Mason, who had been to turn a horse into the same lot, and inquired of him, whether any people were going to work in that pasture in the afternoon, and was answered in the negative.

That the deceased was healthy, cheerful and well, that day, the day before, and always possessed a uniform cheerfulness of spirits. That she was at meeting the day before, and sung with, (though not setting in the same seat with) the singers, and spent a cheerful interim at a friend's near the meeting house; walked home in the afternoon, and arrived home cheerful and gay; and the next day in the forenoon, went through the family business, as usual, with her mother and sister, and was under an engagement, to go abroad in the afternoon, in company with her sister and others, to spend the latter part of the day at Mrs. Marshes.

That, before one o'clock, she went to Mrs. Guild's, eighty rods from her father's house, and tarried there until two o'clock, cheerful and well, and came away, gay as usual. And, at three o'clock, or some few minutes after, her mother, wondering at her stay, looked out for her, and saw the prisoner coming up to the house, covered with blood, with a bloody knife in his hand.

That on the alarm being given, Nehemiah Fales, the deceased's father, and Samuel Fales, ran to the place where the deceased lay, about seventy rods from the house, and in Mason's pasture, and there found her, yet alive, but wounded as is described in the Indictment, and breathing through the wound in her throat, where she expired in a few moments.—The great coat the Prisoner had on, as he was going to the pasture, and his pocket-book, were found near the body. The certificate was found by her feet, torn in pieces, and bloody. Her shoes and shawl off, and at a few feet distance from her. The knife he had in his hand would be proved to be borrowed that morning of one Hardy, and had not been returned. The wounds in the breast, back, and side, agreed with the size of the knife.

Discussion Ideas
for the Classroom

1. What motivates the men in Abingdon to ask Alexander Smyth to prepare this material for publication?

2. How do Virginians in 1806 evaluate material from print culture differently than they regard information from oral culture?

3. What are the traits of a respectable woman in this environment? What defines masculinity?

4. How does law at the local level in this case differ from the proceedings of the district court?

5. How does race affect the events shown here? How might the outcome of the case have been different if John Deskins had been a slave or a free black man? Or if Sidney Hanson had been a slave or a free black woman?

6. What role does alcohol play in this case?

7. In what ways might Smyth have intended the mention of Jason Fairbanks's murder of Elizabeth Fales to affect the jurors?

8. How does social interaction differ by social class in this community? What defines class in this time and place? Would an elite Tidewater woman likely have experienced the diverse race, class, and gender interactions that Sidney Hanson faces in her backcountry social setting?

9. What can the case tell us about the economy of the time?

10. Why would a local historian prefer to purge a rape case from the community's historical memory?

11. How do judicial procedures followed in 1806 differ from procedures followed today? Are there similarities between then and now in how lawyers and witnesses evaluate the truthfulness of the alleged victim and the alleged rapist?

12. How might Smyth's document be treated differently by scholars of various historical fields, such as legal history, gender history, political history, southern history, Appalachian studies, literature, and so on?

Suggested Reading

In light of the lived experience captured in this narrative, scholarly dichotomies can begin to blur. Sharp contrasts—local control versus centralizing structures, respectable citizens versus vagabond ruffians, honor versus law, oral culture versus print culture—grow fuzzy. But these analytical ideas establish the terms by which to analyze the events in Smyth's narrative. The following studies illuminate the context needed for clear-eyed analysis.

The conflict between local cultures of law aimed at maintaining order and a more standardized culture of codified state law has been developed brilliantly in A. G. Roeber, *Faithful Magistrates and Republican Lawyers: Creators of Virginia Legal Culture, 1680–1810* (Chapel Hill: University of North Carolina Press, 1981), and Laura Edwards, *The People and Their Peace: Legal Culture and the Transformation of Inequality in the Postrevolutionary South* (Chapel Hill: University of North Carolina Press, 2009). Vital relevant work on the history of rape and the legal system in early America includes Martha Hodes, *White Women, Black Men: Illicit Sex in the Nineteenth-Century South* (New Haven, Conn.: Yale University Press, 1997); Diane Miller Sommerville, *Rape and Race in the Nineteenth-Century South* (Chapel Hill: University of North Carolina Press, 2004); and Sharon Block, *Rape and Sexual Power in Early America* (Chapel Hill: University of North Carolina Press, 2006). For a study of the Massachusetts murder case mentioned by Smyth, see Dale H. Freeman, "'Melancholy Catastrophe!': The Story of Jason Fairbanks and Elizabeth Fales," *Historical Journal of Massachusetts* 26 (Winter 1998): 1–26. For exemplary use of context and imagination to analyze a little-documented rape in 1638, see Wendy Anne Warren, "'The Cause of Her Grief': The Rape of a Slave in Early New England," *Journal of American History* 93 (March 2007): 1031–49. For more context on law and sexuality in the South, also see Peter W. Bardaglio, *Reconstructing the Household: Families, Sex, and the Law in the Nineteenth-Century South* (Chapel Hill: University of North Carolina Press, 1995), part 1; Joshua D. Rothman, *Notorious in the Neighborhood: Sex and Families across the Color Line in Virginia, 1787–1861* (Chapel Hill: University of North Carolina Press, 2003); John Ruston Pagan, *Anne Orthwood's Bastard: Sex and Law in Early Virginia* (New York: Oxford University Press, 2003); Cynthia A. Kierner, *Scandal at Bizarre: Rumor and Reputation in Jefferson's Virginia* (New York: Palgrave Macmillan, 2004); Fay A. Yarbrough, "Power, Perception, and Interracial Sex: Former Slaves Recall a Multiracial South," *Journal of Southern History* 71 (August 2005): 559–88; and Eva Sheppard Wolf, *Almost Free: A Story about Family and Race in Antebellum Virginia* (Athens: University of Georgia Press, 2012). For the Appalachian context in general, see the early chapters of John Alexander Williams, *Appalachia: A History* (Chapel Hill: University of North Carolina Press, 2002), and David Hsiung, *Two Worlds in the Tennessee Mountains: Exploring the Origins of Appalachian Stereotypes* (Lexington: University Press of Kentucky, 1997).

For more on the broader gender ideologies shaping the place of white women in southern society in the first half of the nineteenth century, see Jan Lewis, *The Pursuit of Happiness: Family and Values in Jefferson's Virginia* (New York: Cambridge University Press, 1983); Suzanne Lebsock, *The Free Women of Petersburg: Status and Culture in a Southern Town, 1784–1860* (New York: Norton, 1984); Stephanie McCurry, *Masters of Small Worlds: Yeoman Households, Gender Relations, and the Political Culture of the Antebellum South Carolina Low Country* (New York: Oxford University Press, 1995); and Cynthia A. Kierner, *Beyond the Household: Women's Place in the*

Early South, 1700–1835 (Ithaca, N.Y.: Cornell University Press, 1998).

The importance of honor to southern men—that is, having a good reputation in the eyes of their peers—has been studied at great length. The classic work is Bertram Wyatt-Brown, *Southern Honor: Ethics and Behavior in the Old South* (New York: Oxford University Press, 1982), but it should be supplemented by Robert Elder, *The Sacred Mirror: Evangelicalism, Honor, and Identity in the Deep South, 1790–1860* (Chapel Hill: University of North Carolina Press, 2016), and David T. Moon Jr., "Southern Baptists and Southern Men: Evangelical Perceptions of Manhood in Nineteenth-Century Georgia," *Journal of Southern History* 81 (August 2015): 563–606. For a perceptive study of the long-lasting informal sanction of men's use of violence to police women's chastity, see Hendrik Hartog, "Lawyering, Husbands' Rights, and 'the Unwritten Law' in Nineteenth-Century America," *Journal of American History* 84 (June 1997): 67–96. For a sense of the social dislocation of many southerners experiencing mobility in the upper South at the turn of the nineteenth century, see John B. Boles, *The Great Revival: Beginnings of the Bible Belt*, new ed. (Lexington: University Press of Kentucky, 1996). On the declining anti-Catholicism of the time, see Chris Beneke, "'Not by Force or Violence': Religious Violence, Anti-Catholicism, and Rights of Conscience in the Early National United States," *Journal of Church and State* 54 (March 2012): 5–32.

The violent and unstable world of the lowest levels of southern society—think of laborers and tenants such as James Bradley, Frederick Trent, and Henry Mash—has been studied insightfully in David Brown, "A Vagabond's Tale: Poor Whites, Herrenvolk Democracy, and the Value of Whiteness in the Late Antebellum South," *Journal of Southern History* 79 (November 2013): 799–840; Keri Leigh Merritt, "'A Vile, Immoral, and Profligate Course of Life': Poor Whites and the Enforcement of Vagrancy Laws in Antebellum Georgia," in *Southern*

Society and Its Transformations, 1790–1860, edited by Susanna Delfino, Michele Gillespie, and Louis M. Kyriakoudes (Columbia: University of Missouri Press, 2011), 25–44; Jeff Forret, *Race Relations at the Margins: Slaves and Poor Whites in the Antebellum Southern Countryside* (Baton Rouge: Louisiana State University Press, 2006); Charles C. Bolton and Scott P. Culclasure, eds., *The Confessions of Edward Isham: A Poor White Life of the Old South* (Athens: University of Georgia Press, 1998); Charles C. Bolton, *Poor Whites of the Antebellum South: Tenants and Laborers in Central North Carolina and Northeast Mississippi* (Durham, N.C.: Duke University Press, 1994); Bill Cecil-Fronsman, *Common Whites: Class and Culture in Antebellum North Carolina* (Lexington: University Press of Kentucky, 1992); Victoria E. Bynum, *Unruly Women: The Politics of Social and Sexual Control in the Old South* (Chapel Hill: University of North Carolina Press, 1992); and Elliott J. Gorn, "'Gouge and Bite, Pull Hair and Scratch': The Social Significance of Fighting in the Southern Backcountry," *American Historical Review* 90 (February 1985): 18–43. On differentiating between poor whites and more prosperous yeomen, such as the Hansons, see Samuel C. Hyde Jr., "*Plain Folk* Reconsidered: Historiographical Ambiguity in Search of Definition," *Journal of Southern History* 71 (November 2005): 803–30, and Samuel C. Hyde Jr., ed., *Plain Folk of the South Revisited* (Baton Rouge: Louisiana State University Press, 1997).

Index

New Directions in Southern History

Series Editors
Michele Gillespie, Wake Forest University
William A. Link, University of Florida

CPSIA information can be obtained
at www.ICGtesting.com
Printed in the USA
BVOW11s0303060217
475321BV00001B/2/P